The Pitfalls of Speculation

BY

Thomas Gibson

FRASER PUBLISHING COMPANY
Burlington, Vermont

Originally published in 1906
by The Moody Corporation

Fraser Publishing Company Edition, 1994
    a division of Fraser Management Associates
    Box 494
    Burlington VT 05402

Library of Congress Catalog Card Number: 94-71678

ISBN: 0-87034-114-6

Printed in the United States of America

CONTENTS

"So great are the opportunities offered by speculative changes, that, with proper methods and self control, the poor man cannot afford to overlook them."

I

Introduction

The Public Attitude Toward Speculation

THE public attitude toward speculation is generally hostile. Even those who venture frequently are prone to speak discouragingly of speculative possibilities, and to point warningly to the fact that an overwhelming majority of speculative commitments result in loss, while those who venture not at all, and consequently are incompetent to judge, dismiss the subject with the statement that marginal trading is gambling, pure and simple, and is therefore pernicious.

Those who enter into the subject a little farther, and attempt to adduce more specific argument against speculative possibilities, lay stress upon the statement that manipulation, trickery and wholesale deception render it impossible for the outsider to enter the field safely or intelligently. These statements, usually unsupported, and frequently insupportable, are accepted by the prejudiced multitude as gospel truth, without any attempt being made to examine their foundation or correctness.

So far as the question of gambling is concerned, it would be entering a very large field to attempt to define just what is and what is not gambling.

The idea that the man who buys a certain stock outright invests, while he who buys on margin gambles, is a popular fallacy. The speculator purchases in the hope of an advance, and if two purchases are made for parallel reasons, one for cash, and one on margins, both purchases are speculative.

That speculative fluctuations are largely used as a basis for gambling operations, is unquestionably true, and possibly an acceptable dividing line may be drawn on the following hypothesis: gambling, in the general acceptance of the term, is founded upon blind chance, the equal possibility of certain events occurring or not occurring; this is modified in some cases by the exercise of superior skill in such games as admit of skill; but fundamentally, gambling is wholly dependent upon the equal chances of two or more opposed individuals.

The trader, therefore, who takes "flyers"

with no knowledge of his subject, or the properties in which he deals, merely gambles on the ultimate rise and fall of the market; but the trader, who, after careful investigation and study, purchases a property, either outright or on margins, because he has reasons for believing it to be cheap, and that it will enhance in value, is a speculator.

Those composing the gambling element are in the majority, and it is needless to say, are the greatest losers; in fact their losses foot up almost the sum total of speculative deficiency, and consequently the sum total of the gains reaped by the real speculator.

The statement that most public commitments are made on no better foundation than a mere guess, may seem a trifle bold, and the counter statement may be made that few people purchase a stock without some reason for so doing. This is admitted on the same basis that the man who bets on a certain number at roulette because it has not recently appeared, or in hope of an immediate repetition, considers that he has a reason for his action. Thus a great number of amateur, or semi-professional traders, buy a certain commodity for no better reason than that the stock has declined, or, more frequently, from a participation in a period of speculative intoxication. They can give reasons for their ventures, but they are without foundation, and are no more worthy of consideration than the reasons given by the roulette player for "staking" upon a certain number.

On the other hand, the speculator, with a carefully acquired knowledge of the normal value of certain properties, fully posted on conditions in general, and those affecting, or liable to affect his favorite property in particular, patiently waits the opportunity to buy, not at a normal price, but at a price far below the actual value of his property. He knows that speculative prices move in cycles, more or less pronounced and prolonged, and in the revolution of this cycle he will be given an opportunity not only to purchase at a price far below a normal valuation, but to sell at a price far above it.

This looks simple enough in the telling, and is merely the operation of Anselm Rothschild's famous advice, "buy cheap and sell dear." But when the statement is made that over 90% of public purchases are made at the approximate high tide of a market and about the same percentage of sales at the approximate low tide, in short, that the most simple and reasonable methods of making money are not only disregarded, but actually reversed, a great field for analysis and discussion presents itself.

Manipulation and trickery are vastly overestimated: popular prejudice continually accords to such causes events which were brought about almost wholly by the composite folly of public participators in speculative affairs, and which could not possibly have been effected by any individual interests.

That these stages of undue depression and inflation are to some extent assisted by the shrewd minority, is true; but the great work is that of the public itself.

That the money-making minority foresee, and take advantage of these extremes, is unquestionable. They are the cause of all speculative movements of importance, and through the errors and losses of the lambs the accumulations of successful operators are made possible.

After a careful examination, covering a period of ten years, and a study of the methods of successful and unsuccessful traders as shown in some thousands of speculative accounts, the following facts are adduced:

1st—The greatest causes of loss in speculation are ignorance, over-speculation, and carelessness, of importance in the order named.

2nd—The popular fallacy that business methods are not applicable to speculation is wholly erroneous.

3rd—Not one speculator in a thousand applies ordinary business precautions to his trades, nor founds his ventures upon knowledge of any value.

4th—The correct trader has little to fear, and much to gain from manipulative tactics.

5th—While extremes of prices move in irregular cycles, no "system" for judging changes is possible, or tenable, as such mechanical attempts to forecast price changes do not contemplate changed conditions, or provide for accident. The advocates of the "Chart System" are legion, and yet it is impossible to find a single permanent and substantial gain made by this method.

6th—The general idea that the actual value, and probable future of a property cannot be intelligently based, is erroneous.

7th—The greatest speculative profits are made in stocks, and the greatest speculative losses, in staples: wheat, corn, cotton, etc.

8th—There are certain technical stages, or conditions of markets which are followed by certain invariable results, the study and recognition of which is valuable, and not difficult. These "ear-marks" are in some cases very plain, and do not in any way smack of the "systems" deprecated above, but are more or less visible signs of effects following certain causes.

9th—Almost every general idea of speculation is the exact reverse of the truth. Sometimes this is caused by false reasoning, but most frequently by the innate false appearance of the market quotations. For example, greatest activity and interest in a market occurs around top prices; while dulness and stagnation are invariable when properties are unreasonably low in price.

10th—Persistent short selling of stocks is fashionable in a certain class of semi-professional traders, and almost invariably results in loss.

11th—Tips are illogical. Any wide-spread dissemination of advance information as to a projected movement would defeat its own object. The so-called "tip'" is usually mere guess work. The general consensus of public opinion on this subject is correct, i. e., tips are valueless; and yet the public continues to use them largely as a basis of trading.

12th—Too great facilities for obtaining information and executing orders, is, to the ordinary trader, of no advantage, and is frequently a source of loss. (The accounts mentioned above show the most intelligent trading to have been done by traders who were without facilities to interfere with their own original plans through fright or confusion.)

13th—Speculation is a safe business when business methods are applied to it. The changes in prices of standard properties offer yearly greater opportunities for profit than any other field. That is to say, for reasonable profits, not for the amassing of fortunes on small capital, in a brief period, but for steady accumulation of money and valuable knowledge. So great are the opportunities offered by speculative changes, that with proper methods and self-control, the poor man cannot afford to overlook them.

To make these rather radical statements in a general way is wholly insufficient; each statement must be supported by the presentation of convincing precedent and clear reasoning, and it is the purpose of these articles to point out the reasons for the failure of the majority, as well as the methods by which the minority succeed. This done, the knowledge so gained must be insulated into useful channels, and combined into flexible rules, and inflexible laws.

It is not claimed that it is possible to set down in print a formula for speculative success: much depends upon the individual. A man is not a machine, and will be frequently swerved into paths which he, himself, knows to be dangerous, and an individual incapable of clear thinking and correct application of accrued knowledge, would not succeed at this, or any other business.

The most that may be hoped for, consequently, is to point out certain facts which will lead to a correct line of thinking, or open the way to profitable discussion. To this end, the various causes of loss mentioned will be discussed in turn.

II

Ignorance, Over-Speculation, Etc.

IGNORANCE, over-speculation, and the innate false appearance of market stages are the principal causes of speculative loss, and are, in truth, the principal causes of the great cycles of speculative extremes. These extremes are variously attributed to specific causes, affecting certain securities, to good or bad business conditions, or to accident or manipulation; but the fact of the matter is that the wide swings of the market are brought about almost wholly by the errors and ignorance of the great body of traders known as the public.

Conditions change, accidents occur, and manipulation exists, and all have their effect; but unless these factors were supplemented by alternate waves of general over-confidence, and subsequent undue depression, the fluctuations in market quotations for standard properties would be confined to such narrow limits that the repeated opportunities to purchase such properties at prices far below, and to sell

them at prices far above a normal value, would
be eliminated.

Almost all the commitments made by public
traders are made on faith, or on misleading
surface appearances. The advice of people
absolutely incapable of passing intelligent
opinions, is eagerly listened to and frequently
acted upon; large dividends on low-priced
stocks are made the basis of optimistic views
and shallow arguments; the fact that a certain
stock has dragged back in a generally strong
market,—usually the best evidence in the
world of something radically wrong with that
particular stock,—incites what may be very
undesirable purchases. The development of
certain long-heralded events, such as the payment, or increase of a dividend, is considered
a good reason for the purchase of the security
affected, when in fact it is no reason at all, as
Wall Street always anticipates and discounts
probable good news. These and a hundred and
one other reasons, mostly ill-founded, are the
groundwork of the great bulk of public ventures, and the individuals who operate on these
unreliable signs, with full knowledge of the
fact that the public has been misled by them
time and again, seldom attempt to investigate
the intrinsic value of the property in which

they have assumed and paid cash for a proprietary interest. Such an investigation is usually considered useless or impossible. If this were true any participation whatever in speculative affairs would be folly, but fortunately this common opinion is itself the result of ignorance.

Over-speculation, the composite result of ignorance, greed, and false appearances, may be classed as the primary cause of wide variations in prices, for as much too high as a market is carried by rash participation at high prices, just as much too low will it sink in the ensuing decline. The ill-advised traders who rush in at high prices with inadequate capital are the first to suffer; their overthrow topples over other weak accounts, and so on down the line, until the last of the wobbly row of bricks has fallen.

It might be contended that when this process of elimination had brought prices of good properties to a fair valuation, purchasers would be easily found, and such might be the case, were it not for the fact that the great lights of speculative finance know full well that the technical position of the market is still bad; that many venturers, already financially weakened by the decline from abnormal to normal prices, are in a position which they can be forced to abandon; that the pendulum of prices will swing to the other extreme, and they refrain from buying at normal prices for the good and simple reason that they know they can eventually buy at prices that are very low. Perhaps these low prices will come about unaided, through the internal rottenness of the technical situation; perhaps the desirable consummation will require a little assistance, such as the passing of a dividend or two, the closing of a few mills or the laying off of a few men, all of which actions can in the future be pointed out as good and conservative business moves, but which will be received by the public with anger and disgust; for so dense is general ignorance on this one subject that the payment of a dividend is always considered good, and the reduction or passing of a dividend is always considered bad; a bond issue, for whatever purpose, is an unmixed evil, and so following.

The professional bear element also assists in the final downfall of prices. They will be well aware of the assailable condition of the weakened long interest, and will attack the market for the purpose of reaching stop-loss orders or forcing crippled speculators to sell. These same bears may later be hoist with their

own petard, for a chronic bear is a chronic
loser, but meanwhile they assist the successful
campaigners materially by forcing a temporarily lower level of prices and supplanting
weak long accounts with a short interest,
which is in itself a great advantage to the bull
element.

So familiar is the experienced speculator
with public weakness that he is usually found
operating in direct reversion to prevailing sentiment. He knows by careful and clear-headed
investigation the normal value of the property
or properties in which he trades, and at such
time as he finds the current quotations far below this fixed point and the public inveighing
bitterly against his favorite issues, he begins
his purchases. It does not require much
shrewdness to deduce the fact that if a certain
standard security has passed out of public, or
weak hands, it has of necessity been concen-
trated in the strong hands of the giants of
finance, and that the purchaser at such periods
is at least in good company. He has no fear of
any abnormal shrinkage in the value of his
holdings, as such sudden shrinkages are the
result of panic or financial necessity, to which
the present holders are not subject. He also
knows that any manipulation must now be for

the purpose of creating higher prices, as the next great speculative move will be to resell the cheaply purchased properties at high prices, and the public being absent, there is no one to manipulate against. He is certain that unless all precedents fail, he will, at some future time, see high prices and general good feeling supplant the present depression.

As has been stated, the innate false appearance of speculative surroundings does much to influence public participation at the wrong period. When stocks are low in price the brokerage offices are deserted, the newspapers say little of speculative affairs, transactions are limited, and those who have been worsted in the preceding decline speak in pessimistic terms of the future. A long period of dullness almost invariably follows a severe decline, new lambs must be born and the old ones suffered to grow a new fleece, and dullness is always unattractive. But at the crest of a great movement all is activity. Excited groups gather about the tickers and predict future events founded principally on illusions or hope, and stories of quickly acquired gains are heard on every hand. A fever of speculation fills the air and men who had no thought of venturing during the time of depression and low prices, now purchase anything and everything at prices that are very high.

The mistakes discussed above—ignorance; the belief that speculative riches are the result of luck rather than of judgment, over-speculation and misleading surface appearances, combine to make it possible for the shrewd and successful minority to buy and sell periodically to great advantage by an almost exact reversal of public methods and beliefs. Their operations are not founded on such reversion, but on study and knowledge of past precedent, present conditions and future probabilities. The fact that public opinion is diametrically opposed to their views may be cheerfully considered as excellent proof of the correctness of their deductions, as the public is usually wrong.

If the statements made above are admitted to be correct the lesson they teach is obvious. To result successfully, speculative ventures must be based on sound reasoning and a knowledge of correct normal values; on a willingness to confine operations to reasonable limits and upon emancipation from the moving influences of general exhiliration or depression. The individual who begins or pursues his operations on these great fundamental principles has taken a great step toward the goal of success.

III

Manipulation

THERE are two classes of manipulative tactics indulged in by the inside workers of Wall Street; the long range tactics of the great but silent workers who lay a plan contemplating a complete speculative cycle from high to low prices, and the more frequent and drastic operations of room traders who find a market in a bad technical position and operate for known effects, either as a matter of immediate profit or to rid themselves of a dangerous following. The success of both is dependent upon public folly.

In the first class lies the hidden and carefully calculated work of haute finance. It consists of creating, or helping to create, false impressions as to the value of a certain property, of lending encouragement to buy at high prices, or to sell (or at least to refrain from buying), at low prices. The motives are obvious: to create a demand for the goods for sale, and to create a supply of the goods whose purchase is contemplated.

This high form of financiering is always helped by shrewd choosing of propitious periods and surroundings, and its moving factors, though potent with result, are so veiled and untraceable as to render supportable criticism impossible.

The recent price movements of the properties of the United States Steel Corporation furnish a pointed example of this method of financiering. The stocks were offered to the public at prices which were really fair, statements were issued which were unquestionably correct, and dividends were paid which were doubtless earned. The periodical reports were rosy, but they were true. The great earnings were made, and called attention to the high tide of a period of unusual activity and prices, but the public did not take the trouble to ascertain this important fact. They saw only one thing, that large dividends were being paid, and still larger earnings being carried to surplus, by a company whose stocks were selling at low prices. They looked neither backward nor forward, but glued their eyes upon the insufficient facts of the present. A little knowledge would have proven that not only were the recent and present earnings unusually large, but that all such abnormal periods are followed by a reaction.

These simple facts, known and recognized in the abstract as being true of all businesses, were lost in the greed and fever of speculation. Knowledge and study played no part in the affair; the present was all-sufficient, and the public bought largely, both for investment and on margins; and by the same token, the promoter sold. Later the earnings fell off, which was perfectly natural, money was lavishly disbursed, their holdings increased by the purchase of new properties; the surplus dwindled, and dividends on the common stock were reduced and eventually suspended altogether.

A public change of heart took place, and views of the company's future changed from extreme rosiness to cross-grained cynicism. Again the present was made the only standard; the stock was watered; the common shares were absolutely worthless; future dividends were impossible, etc.

The fact that a great deal of money had been intelligently diverted into channels which could not but enhance the future value of the corporation was not considered, and so, during a natural period of reaction, the disgusted public gradually relinquished their holdings, and they passed back, little by little, into the hands of their original owners at prices ridiculously low.

From the standpoint of the great manipulators, it was beautifully done. Not one argument could be brought against them which could not be amply defended. "We paid dividends because we earned them, and you, our stock-holders, clamored for them and approved of them; we gave to the world statements of every dollar received and disbursed; nothing was misrepresented, nothing was concealed. When the iron and steel business suffered a relapse, and our surplus had been lowered by excellent and necessary expenditures, we did what every business man does—decreased our expenses and our dividends until an improvement was apparent. We are not responsible for the actions of Wall Street, and if you, as an individual, made ill-advised purchases and sales, or over-speculated, that is no fault of ours. Yes, we did, as individuals, sell some stocks at prices which we considered fair, and likewise re-purchased at prices which are considered low. That was a matter of business, and was our privilege. We have absolute confidence in our properties and their future and

always have had. You cannot blame us for
your mistakes; you beat yourselves; get out!"

This is unanswerable, but the fact remains
that these men knew what the effect of their
actions would be and acted accordingly. No
one who has a personal acquaintance with Mr.
Morgan and his principal lieutenants would
harbor any thought of their having participated
in the general enthusiasm, and making the
error of themselves believing there would be
no reaction in the large earnings and good
condition of the affairs of the Steel Corporation. Never.

That they had faith in their properties is
literally true, and it is doubtful if the largest
holders would have parted so freely with their
stocks but that they knew absolutely what
would happen, and that the stocks would per-
force be returned to them at low prices.
Neither did they find it necessary to cripple or
permanently injure their great consolidation to
bring about their grand coup. The shares had
the same inherent value at the lowest range,
as at the highest.

It is unquestionably true that if the mag-
nates "who never speculate" had not foreseen
and acted upon public folly, no dividends
would have been paid which could not have

been maintained, and instead of the wild pyro-
technics and wide-price range of steel stocks,
the properties would have steadily increased
in value from the birth of the concern.

There is nothing new in all this—it is a time-
honored method of speculative financiering,
from the repetition of which the public seems to
learn nothing, and from which the most powerful interests make their largest returns.

The second class of manipulation, more
recognizable as such, is more brief as to period
and more restricted as to results, but is potent
enough at times to bring about changes and
appearances which either force or frighten
holders out of a good position, or mislead them
into a bad one.

The cry is frequently heard that the public
is not in the market, and this state of affairs is
usually pointed out as a reason for stocks not
advancing. This view is another evidence of
the reversed reasoning so prevalent in speculative matters.

The very last thing the great speculators
want in the market is such an interest at low
prices, or even at midway points in an advance.
So undesirable, in fact, is such an element that
its presence means defeat for the sponsors of
the deal themselves, and a projected movement

is sometimes abandoned temporarily on account of too large a following. The most approved method, however, is to "shake out" and discourage this following. The process is simple; the great inside element finding themselves in company of numerous "tailers," whose weakness and liability to panic on the slightest pretext may ruin their own devices, take advantage of just such known weakness, and with the assistance of the professional bears, proceed to drive their undesirable friends away. To accomplish this, support is withdrawn and a portion of the accumulated holdings sold ostentatiously. The bear element, fully aware of the assailable state of the market, assists the manipulators by heavy sales and vicious drives. The enthusiastic public, crippled, discouraged and disgusted, drop their holdings, and a considerable number of half-baked bears join in the same game of "follow the leader," until a short interest is created. Meanwhile, the original projectors replace their holdings at opportune times, perhaps at a lower average than that at which their spectacular sales were made, perhaps not—but the physicking has been accomplished, the atmosphere is cleared, and the "deal" which they had never for a moment contemplated abandoning, goes merrily on until such time as another purging may be necessary.

These two forms of speculative tactics, with their various off-shoots, constitute the fundamental basis of manipulation. They are widely different; the one, the long distance work of the great "financier" who pays no heed to ordinary movements, but works toward a great end; the other, the tactics of purely speculative interests. The first is responsible for the long swing of the market; the second for many of its sharp intermediate changes; but both are united in one thing, they work together for the undoing of the general public.

The man who invests, or speculates for the long swing may, like the first class, disregard all ordinary hippodroming, and await certain results.

The man who indulges more freely in speculative ventures must bring to his aid clear thinking, study and vigilance. Above all things he must provide for sharp changes financially, and if he is caught in a flurry, his embarrassment will be only temporary.

In both cases everything depends upon an intelligent basis of normal valuation, for to that basis, if correctly estimated, the price of his holdings will eventually revert.

All the manipulation, accident and trickery in the world can not keep prices too low nor too high for long. The needle of the compass may be disturbed and swing nervously from side to side, but it must point to the true north at last.

IV

Accidents

ACCIDENTS or unexpected events frequently mark the beginning of sharp or extended declines. It is generally considered that anything in the nature of an accident must be in favor of the bear element.

This theory in the abstract is sound enough, as accident and disaster are nearly synonymous, but careful consideration of the subject will develop the fact that in the speculative world accidents are more frequently the excuse for, than the cause of, any severe or extended decline, and their effects are to be measured by the stage and condition of the market, rather than by their actual capacity for evil.

Nothing in the nature of the unforeseen can be conceived as happening which could permanently injure or retard the growth and value of good properties.

The United States has such recuperative power that the naturally increasing value of her properties can easily overcome the temporary effects of unforeseen occurrences. It is reasonable to believe that if all the accidents which have occurred and have been pointed out as the cause of great market changes in the last ten years had never happened, stocks would still be at the same approximate level as they are today.

It is admitted that accidents frequently administer the little shove to an already bad state of affairs which hastens a decline that must have eventually and inevitably occurred, accident or no accident. This is not wholly an unmixed evil, as it may be the means of checking excesses, which, if allowed to continue, might result in even more severe consequences.

On the other hand, an accident may sometimes mark the very beginning of a great upward movement by frightening from the market at low prices weak and foolish speculators whose very presence spells danger, and attracting to it far-seeing men who gauge prices by values.

The danger of adverse litigation, (which may be classed among unforseen events), against good properties is slight. Annually, numerous tirades are begun against combinations and individual corporations in the legislative halls, or in the columns of the public press, supplemented by the railing of the notoriety-seeking charlatans who find it popular to inveigh against capital in general, but the fact remains that no measures will be taken, or at least no measures can endure, that will prevent the builders of railroads, or the capitalizers of great industries from making good returns on their money, or from seeing their investments grow in value through the advance of demand and population. Such measures, expounded by dreamers, or socialistic tin-horn tooters, strike at the very foundation of business extension, and per contra, any individual or coterie of individuals, who seek to overdo the extension of capital, or make it bring exorbitant and unnatural returns, will, like the toad in the fable, burst by self-inflation.

Stripped of these two extremes, business conditions are sound and solid, and gradual growth and prosperity are assured.

The unexpected calling of loans, the exportation of gold, the killing of crops, sharp changes in the attitude of foreign markets, etc., are matters which are to be expected annually, either as natural or manipulated events under any and all conditions, and are almost wholly impotent to change the course of a long swing to high or low prices. Like the boy who cried "Wolf, Wolf," on every occasion, they lose their importance by repetition.

True, these minor signs may to the close student sometimes appear as straws indicating the course of the financial wind, but generally speaking, nothing short of a wide-spread and severe disaster can change the course of the great cycles of speculation, the repeated and unchecked revolutions of the wheel of fortune.

A good illustration of the statement that accidents frequently prove merely the puff of wind which topples over an already rotten structure, is found in the death of the late R. P. Flower. This unexpected occurrence was followed by a radical and extended decline in the properties known as the "Flower Stocks." It cannot be reasonably claimed that the cancellation of Mr. Flower's personality affected the securities in question, as the number of stocks in the group, and the fact that he had no voice in the affairs of some of his favorites, combined to render any personal direction of the internal workings of the properties involved, impossible. His personal efforts, for instance, could not have sustained Brooklyn Rapid Transit above par; the stock was not, and never has been worth the prices at which it sold. It may, probably will, at some future day be cheap at that figure, but at the time in question, the price was premature, if not ridiculous. What followed Mr. Flower's demise must have occurred from its own inherent weakness, sooner or later; the event simply hastened the inevitable.

It is not the intention in the above illustration to cast any aspersions upon the methods or memory of the financier; he was sincere, but an enthusiast. He told his friends certain things would happen, and believed they would. His speculative campaign attracted to him a large and dangerous following, and his views of values were based more upon optimism than reason. He was honest, but he was mistaken.

The death of a great financier is always considered for its probable market effect, which must, of course, be measured by the actual result. The probability of such an event acting as a fillip to an already over-strained condition may be eliminated on the theory that in such cases they become excuses, not causes. It is not reasonable to believe that the removal of any one man from the financial map will be followed by any sustained depression. The affairs of such men almost invariably revert to

good hands by direct succession, and the popular fallacy about rich men's sons is being continually disproved by such men as the Vanderbilts, George Gould, and Ogden Armour.

Mr. Gould's death was, if anything, a boon to
the speculative world; he was a trickster and
a wrecker; his son is a "builder-up." Even in
the improbable event of a great financier
dying intestate his holdings would quickly find
a resting place in strong hands at their true
value.

The danger of wide-spread epidemic has
always been regarded as a bear point, and were
it not for the fact that the advance of science
and the improvement in sanitary conditions
now invariably confines even the most contagious and virulent diseases to limited areas,
the devastations of a plague might be seriously
regarded. As it is, the probability of any material damage from such a source is remote,
and the bears, wont to welcome with open
arms, ruin, devastation and death, have almost
discarded them as weapons.*

The most serious of all events classed as
accidents, is war, with its heavy entail and

*In the cholera scare of 1892, when the "yellow flag," in-
dicating cholera on board, was shown outside the New York
harbor, an excited bear rushed upon the floor of the Exchange,
shouting, "Hurrah, hurrah, the cholera is here." He was
suspended.

general disruption of affairs. That our country will not be plunged into a disastrous or
prolonged war must be taken on faith, and the
struggles of other nations, in which we are not
involved, is productive of more good than evil;
as, while it may bring about the forced selling
of some of our securities held abroad, it also
places the United States in the position of a
huckster, and makes a market for our products
at materially higher prices, which prosperous
condition must be reflected in all lines of business. No better example of this could be given
than the recent struggle between Russia and
Japan.

The contention is therefore made that while
accident is frequently made the excuse for
speculative declines, it is seldom the cause, and
that if conditions are sound and prices low, any
sharp decline brought about by unforseen hap-
penings creates opportunities which would
otherwise not have existed. On the occasion
of public fright at such stages, it is frequently
the case that great men come to the "assistance" of the market, and buy stocks heavily,
(when they are low enough), and are hailed as
public benefactors. That such purchases are
made from purely philanthropic motives is, to
say the least, doubtful.

The speculator, therefore, who has mapped out a well-formed plan of operation, can afford to ignore the probability, or possibility of accident, except to provide for any sudden flurry occasioned by such causes; or, if an active operator, may sometimes take advantage of unreasonable fright and apprehension to replace, or increase his holdings.

There is no gainsaying the fact that a serious accident or event is possible; but to be effective it must be in the nature of a far-reaching disaster, and may be viewed by the trader with about the same degree of apprehension as he views the danger of being struck by lightning in his daily walks.

V

Business Methods In Speculation

FEW men embark in a business pursuit of any kind without a careful examination of the prospects and environments of their ventures. If a business, or an interest in a business; is to be purchased, the past, present and probable future of that business are carefully examined. The assets and liabilities are compared, the record of past sales and profits are considered, and the probable future of the community, or territory from which the business draws its revenue, is given particular attention, and also, the danger of a decimation of profits through competition is considered. The character of the individuals concerned as partners or managers is weighed, and if found wanting, the proposition is discarded, as confidence between men is the foundation of all successful combinations.

Neither does the prospective purchaser enter his field without some special education for the business in hand, or at least not without a determination to watch and learn daily something of the technicalities of his enterprise.

These simple facts are recognized the world over as merely plain, sensible precautions adopted by all business men in all businesses—all except one—the widely patronized business of speculation.

This disregard of recognized business rules and laws is caused largely by the fact that the multiplicity of speculative properties with their large capitalizations stagger the ordinary mind, and lead a man into the error of considering himself incapable of grappling with so great a problem, and partly by a misplaced confidence in the expressed belief of others.

The opinions of brokers are given a degree of credence to which they are seldom entitled, for, sad to relate, the lack of study and method is almost as prevalent behind the office railing as outside of it, in addition to which the desire to make commissions frequently leads the broker to an expression of encouraging views running parallel with the ideas of the client, whether such views are sincere or not.

The emphatic opinions of friends and acquaintances are also greatly over-rated at times, especially if the advisor has been fortunate in his recent ventures, which fact alone is a dangerous and insufficient guide. This willingness to accept the alleged thinking and knowledge of others frequently results in almost total elimination of thought and knowledge as a basis of operation. It is doubtful if a single case of sustained success in speculative ventures can be pointed out that was not founded upon individual study and investigation.

The idea that large properties cannot be investigated intelligently is a mistake. Every standard listed security must, under the rules of a well conducted exchange, offer to the public every facility for such investigation. The size of a property is only a matter of degree, a multiplication of what represents and belongs to a single share of stock; or, per contra, the value of one share of stock is a division of the whole.

Facts and figures as to assets, earning capacity, territory and past history are easily obtainable,* and the value of the deductions resulting from the thorough and painstaking scrutiny of a property is to be gauged only by individual capacity for clear thinking, stripped of foolish credulity and pig-headed prejudice.

The advantages of choosing for operations

*See The Art of Wall Street Investing.

the standard properties listed upon the New York Stock Exchange are manifold. There is always a market for these properties, which is not true of wild-cat securities; they are admitted to the benefits of the exchange on demonstrated merits, and under inflexible rules. True, a few bad properties have made their way into the exchange, but they have been the exception, not the rule.

The governors of the exchange are men of unquestioned business integrity and honor, and exercise every precaution to exclude undesirable stocks.

It may be contended that the public has been dumped, time and again by the fluctuations of listed stocks, which is exactly true; but that has been the fault of public error, and not of the rules of the stock exchange, nor lack of merit in the properties themselves.

The man who begins his investigations as to the actual value of a listed property, therefore begins with one which holds a high place in the business world, and which certainly has some value. It is his business, therefore, to estimate carefully this value, and upon the result to base his operations.* This knowledge of

---

*The writer's views as to the best method of making such an investigation will appear in a succeeding chapter.

an approximate valuation will prove of great importance, and will materially aid the possessor, and prevent him from undue exhilaration or depression.

He may reasonably argue that all general depression will be followed by improvement, and that every bubble of inflation will be pricked. The United States will take care of itself and all of its good properties.

Matters of moment bearing upon his particular property will, of course, be weighed carefully, and, if of sufficient importance, may necessitate the changing of his basis of valuation, either to a higher or a lower level, but this will be done carefully and slowly.

One thing the investigator may safely consider in his favor, and that one thing is of high importance: that the good properties of a new country are certain to gradually advance in value, with a tendency to restricted fluctuations until final absorption takes place.

This fact is easily explained: a new country offers in the sudden development of its virgin resources opportunities which render fair percentage returns unattractive, and speculative, or even investment capital seeks these channels. But as these opportunities are gradually restricted by development, money seeks the dividend paying properties which will yield perpetual returns.

The man who speculates in a business-like manner will at once see the necessity of entirely eliminating abnormal possibilities and rashness from his plan of operation. The difference between expecting from the market what is reasonable, and expecting too much; and between buying what can be reasonably protected, and even increased, and plunging, is exactly the difference between success and failure.

He who buys one thousand shares of stock on a total capital of ten thousand dollars is ruined before he begins trading. He may succeed once, twice, or twenty times, but his ultimate failure is as certain as death.

Many men with sound ideas, and whose ventures have proved ultimately the correctness of their views, have, by the one fault of overtrading, become paupers, when, with business methods, they might have become millionaires.

It is one of the many strange facts about the great field of opportunity called speculation, that men who consider ten per cent. a good return on capital in ordinary business are wholly dissatisfied with one hundred per cent. in a speculative venture.

The business man in speculation will find it expedient to divorce himself from the alluring attractions of the ticker itself. Many traders whose long range views of values and approaching conditions are good, get their noses so close to the ticker as to shut out the true perspective. They deceive themselves into the belief that they are keeping well posted by haunting the brokerage offices and following the mass of good, bad and indifferent gossip, conflicting opinions, canards, and predictions, as well as being swayed by the innumerable flurries which occur almost daily, and are always accompanied by an excuse. For a man is human, and no matter how phlegmatic by nature or cultivation, is more or less moved by these pernicious influences.

Anything worthy of consideration may better be considered in cold blood, than in the active time and place of speculation, and if commitments have been intelligently made and provided for, propinquity to the ticker will far oftener prove a detriment than an aid to profits. There are no doubt many professional scalpers, whose business is the chasing of fractions, who watch the slightest variation in quotations, and by so doing make some money—a great deal less, by the way, than is popularly supposed—and who find their constant presence at the ticker a necessity to their particular scheme of operation, but these articles are not written for their benefit.

The time spent in gathering a bewildering mass of false impressions, so untrustworthy as to be ridiculous, and so numerous as to be confusing, can be much more profitably spent as every really successful operator spends his time, in study and sound reasoning.

The choosing of a broker is important, financial responsibility and personal integrity being the first considerations. Brokers who offer reductions from the fixed standard of interest and commissions should be regarded with suspicion; such advantages are usually dearly purchased. Standard charges are not unreasonably high, and are not to be considered a drawback if general methods are correct.

A good broker may also frequently aid in the forming of opinions, or in the confirmation of opinions already formed; but as every trader, to succeed, must do his own thinking, this is not of so much importance as is the assurance of stability and probity. It is cold comfort to see one's carefully figured deductions confirmed, and then see the results vanish in the failure of an unreliable house, and yet this same event occurs again and again.

Summing up, the man who speculates in a business-like way trades only in standard properties with whose history, physical condition, earnings and prospects he has thoroughly familiarized himself; forms for himself a careful estimate of normal value and uses this value as a gauge by which to decide when prices are too low and too high; takes into consideration also the technical condition of the market, and does not embark with bad company, even at low prices; is not misled by the thrills of inflation, or the chills of depression; operates, not for the purpose of gathering a small profit from many transactions, but to gather a large profit from a few; trades with responsible middle-men, and, above all things, is patient. In short, he maps out for himself an intelligent and well-founded plan of operation, contemplating all that may occur, and having mapped it out, follows it.

Very few speculate in this manner, and— very few succeed.

VI

Market Technicalities

THE study of technicalities, of which little is generally known, and about which nothing has been written, is of great importance to the speculator, and particularly to the active trader.

The two most glaring, as well as the most important technical appearances which mark the top and bottom of a speculative cycle, have been commented on in a previous chapter; they consist of dullness and stagnation at the bottom of a movement, and crazy recklessness and universal participation at the other extreme.

In addition to the facts that have already been presented in regard to these two extremes, the following rule may be set down:

It is practically impossible for an over-bought market to advance materially, or for an over-sold market to decline materially.

This seemingly radical statement is so well based as to be operative regardless of actual

values. That is to say, if a certain stock is selling at sixty and is intrinsically worth par, it is
very unlikely that it will reach par while there
exists a general marginal participation for the
long account; and on the other hand, a stock
which is selling at par and is worth only sixty,
will not decline if there is a heavy short interest in it.

These statements may at first blush seem
opposed to the previous contention that any
security must eventually seek its correct level;
not so, for the fact is that correct levels will
finally be reached, but not until the preponderance of participating opinion has been equal-
ized; or, what is more common, exactly reversed.

There have been many cases where the better class of traders have made a strong favorite of a certain security, and have been wholly
unable to account for its dullness or depression.
Frequently their original deductions have been
correct, but after long and patient waiting for
the price of the stock to readjust itself to what
they correctly considered its true valuation,
they have withdrawn in disgust, or have even
allowed themselves to believe that there must
be some concealed rottenness about the affairs

of the corporation which they are unable to ferret out.

The analysis of this state of affairs is neither profound nor difficult. First, and most important, is the fact that the buying power which is necessary to any marked advance is absent. The public having made a favorite of the stock, has loaded up and is waiting for an advance. The public buying is completed, and no matter how inviting the proposition may be, so far as intrinsic merit goes, the big men will not buy while this public interest exists. They will not participate in a deal which contemplates a hoi polloi partnership, and aside from this, they are aware of the fact that they can certainly purchase cheaper in time if the present holders are left to their own devices.

In order to pursue any deal looking to an advance in the security in question, the professionals realize that should they enter the lists now they would be working for public benefit. They must not only buy in a restricted market at advancing prices, but must be prepared to take over at higher prices the present holdings of the public.

This is not the method used by great speculators; they do not bid for and assist the public in its speculative affairs, but accept at low prices what the public is throwing away. The professional element therefore cannot be counted on to forward prices. They will wait.

Meanwhile the numerous friends of the stock sit and twiddle their thumbs and wonder what in the world is the matter.

This state of affairs, it is evident, would cure itself in time through the certain and unstoppable assertion of intrinsic merit, but the required time will not be granted by the impatient holders. Something entirely different (and more rapid) will occur. The impatient public will throw over its stocks in disgust one by one, and each decline will confirm others in the belief that there is "something rotten" in the stock. It being impossible to uncover or point out anything detrimental, something is invented, and the well-meant plans of the holders end in a general decline, and after a time, in the hands of people who know both values and methods, the stock is first absorbed, then galvanized into activity, and finally hippodromed back into public hands at prices higher than they had first figured as its value.

The statements made above are not calculated to encourage the public trader. It certainly looks as if he had a hard row to hoe when even intrinsic valuation, correctly estimated, will not always produce satisfactory results; but the knowledge of this important technical condition and its cause and effect will prove of the highest value to the trader. He may reason as follows: I have figured and estimated the value of this security and find it to be too low, but unfortunately it is a public favorite. Its cheapness is so apparent as to attract to it a large following incapable of either patient waiting or sustained action. The widespread nature of these holdings, and the character of the holders render any concerted action for a more or less manipulated advance out of the question. On the other hand, the holders who now believe in the stock will daily grow more impatient at its torpidity, and will eventually begin to liquidate. This will be followed by numerous canards inimical to its price, and the stock will, at the bottom prices, be friendless so far as the public is concerned. When this consummation is reached, the stock will rest in the hands of men who possess all the qualifications of speculative success—patience, money and a full knowledge of how to start the machinery of an advance at the right time.

In following this reasoning the trader is doing exactly what the great inside interests do, and if he refrains from purchasing, even at low prices, when a security is too popular, he may rest assured that he will be able to purchase more cheaply in time. The chances are a hundred to one that no safe or material advance will occur under such conditions. The amateurs and the professionals cannot win on the same side in a speculative deal. It is the survival of the fittest, and the trader can soon decide with which side he wishes to identify himself. On the one hand are narrow margins, over-speculation, absolute lack of method; on the other, wealth, knowledge, concentration, and organization.

These are cold, hard facts and require only the directed exercise of good reasoning to be taken advantage of.

The same rule in inverse ratio applies to an oversold market, except that the danger to the seller is even greater. The professionals, a purely speculative party with whom the greater lights of speculation do not hesitate to ally themselves occasionally, are always on the lookout for an over-sold market, and the squeeze they sometimes administer to a widespread short interest is very severe.

There is nothing in the speculative world more hazardous than short-selling in a numerous company.

In digesting the above statements, the question naturally arises: "How may a bad technical condition be recognized?" This is not so difficult as it might appear.

It is first necessary to lay aside any preconceived personal opinions and prejudices bearing on the stock in question, and conduct inquiries unhampered by "the wish that is father to the thought."

The published opinions and interviews in the newspapers, the expression of opinions among the speculators generally, and if possible, a frank inquiry from a friend at court, viz.: a broker who has means of knowing whether or not a widely scattered and considerable long or short interest exists—will usually prove sufficient.

A successful Western trader for many years gained this information from the books of a single large private wire house in Chicago, and claimed that he found the method an infallible barometer, and that he would frequently find every office of the company's system on one side of a stock, with scarcely a single trade on the other side. This man, whose word there is no reason to doubt, made the interesting statement that at the approximate high prices of Steel Preferred and Amalgamated Copper he found that the long account in these two stocks, representing the operations of a large and indiscriminate public trade, exceeded those of all other stocks combined, without a single short trade, and that later when Steel Preferred had sold below fifty and started on its upward road, there was not one of the hundred offices in the system whose customers were not short of the stock, while the long account was limited to a few scattered trades.

Such a state of affairs is astonishing, and were it not for a realization of the loss and suffering brought about by such widespread folly, it would be laughable.

The wide general swing of a stock market from high to low prices is marked by an almost unvarying set of extraneous appearances which may be used to advantage by the observant trader.

The bottom of the cycle is marked by dullness and a sawing back and forth in narrow limits, with general sympathizing in the entire list. The successful large interests are accumulating stocks by their time honored method of picking up offerings and bidding for nothing. When this extended period of torpidity has left the public sufficiently bare of stocks, and has also created distrust and pessimism, the advance begins.

The beginning of a bull period is almost always marked by the bidding up of a single stock, and is followed by the picking up of one stock after another until the entire list of values has been materially advanced. There is a hazy public idea that a bull movement is accompanied by a general advance which extends to all active securities. This is not shown by any precedent, but on the other hand the culmination of a bull market is marked by just such a general advance. This may be explained by the statement that the genuine and intermediate advance from low prices to the approximate top is more or less assisted and engineered by the inside factors, who, however well fortified in organization and funds, would not be guilty of endangering themselves, (a la public), by attempting too much at once. These interests, therefore, concentrate efforts and capital, and lift their stocks one at a time, probably returning to the first security in time, and again furthering their favorites in rotation. This is the one and only stage of a market in which a considerable number of public traders make money, for the appearance of one stock after another advancing sharply is so glaring that the more or less sophisticated trader learns to recognize the appearance, and to buy a stock the minute he sees it "start," or develop sudden activity. This period is the brief and golden time for the trading element, but alas, they either over-speculate so rashly that the first natural reaction or engineered shake-out lands them bottom side up, or they absolutely refuse to recognize that there is a top to a movement, and are caught with a large line at the highest prices.

As has been stated, the actual culmination is usually marked by a general advance, which means that the public has entered the lists in force, and are buying any thing at any price. This is the exact condition for which the insiders have worked and waited—a broad and general market for their holdings.

Another public idea is that in the course of a bull market from one extreme to the other there are numerous setbacks and shake-outs. There is nothing in history to show that this view is correct; such declines are limited to one or two breaks of importance during the progress of the entire cycle. This mistake of looking for repeated reactions of importance is another factor which works against the public, for, having seen one or two shake-outs follow-

ed by a continuation of the advance, they look
for an indefinite repetition of such action, and
do not recognize the fact that there will eventually be a decline with no subsequent advance.

The question at once asks itself: "How may
the top of the market be discerned, and the
dangers of the eleventh hour be avoided?"
The answer is more or less complex.

It is, of course, necessary above all things to
revert to the estimated and fixed value of the
stocks traded in and to find out how much
above this normal point the securities are selling. This done, common sense, plus prudence,
and minus piggishness, may determine the
question and dictate the time for liquidation.
This action, however, once decided upon must
be adhered to with great rigidity, for thousands of traders who thus take time by the fore-
lock have been dissatisfied afterwards by seeing
a still greater advance in which they had no
interests, and through greed and impatience
have re-entered the lists at a most inopportune
time.

The trader who realizes his profits, and sees
a further advance follow his own withdrawal
from the market, may console himself with the
fact that he has made and secured a profit;
that trying to guess the exact extreme of a

cycle is hazardous, and that the advance which followed his withdrawal is unsound, being founded on speculation rather than valuation.

But this is a digression from the technical phase of the matter. So far as it is possible to judge the culmination of a speculative campaign by extraneous appearances, it may be said that a long period of backing and filling, a swinging back and forth of prices at the approximate high level marks the beginning of the end. This is occasioned by the following facts:

The definition of the "top" of a market is that point at which the great traders have almost in unison decided to unload, and per contra, the public has reached its highest degree of enthusiasm.. At the beginning of this period the insiders possess an enormous aggregate of stocks which must be sold in such a manner as not to break the market. This operation will take weeks, or even months to accomplish, as any precipitate selling would be disastrous. The wise element, therefore, sells all the market will absorb without any severe decline, and ceases selling, or even takes the buying side at the first appearance of "softness." In short they do all they can to maintain a good feeling and high prices, at the same time parting with securities as rapidly as possible.

This statement may convey the impression that the shrewd speculators act in unison. This is true, but not necessarily in the sense that there is any preconceived arrangement between them.. The unison is more or less unconscious, and is founded on the fact that there are only two sides to the market—the right side and the wrong side, and that those of the speculative world who have sufficient wisdom and experience to know what is right are working to the same end, while all the inexperienced or unthinking horde are working on theories diametrically opposed to reason or even probability.

A careful perusal of the above statements will bring out the following stages as the appearance of a speculative cycle:

First, a long period of dullness, then the rocketing of one stock after another until the entire list has been greatly advanced, one or two shake-outs (always accompanied by specious excuses), a renewal of the advance, and finally general participation and a long period of "see-sawing." These, so far as precedent goes, are the earmarks of a bull period, and may be exactly reversed in a long decline, except that in declines the general list is more greatly affected; that is to say, the whole list crumbles at once.

Aside from the fundamental principles considered above there are numerous minor technicalities which are of value to active traders, but are dangerous and not wholly dependable. For instance, the appearance of strength and heavy buying in a certain security in a low and weak market is almost invariably followed by a decided advance in that particular stock. The analogy of this feature is that this unnatural moving against the current shows heavy accumulation for some reason which will probably be developed later. But such an appearance in a high market might mean exactly the reverse, as one stock may be bid up sharply to permit of liquidation in a dozen others under cover of the sympathetic good feeling engendered by the isolated advance.

The minor technicalities are of use only to experienced traders who have every facility for acting upon them, and to enlarge upon them in a work of this character would be to run the risk of being misunderstood, or even of making statements which might be misleading. In view of this fact, and also as they are not of

primary importance, any discussion of them
is omitted.

If the idea has been conveyed in the above
statements that technical conditions or appearances may be made the sole groundwork of
speculative operations, let the impression be at
once corrected. That these appearances and
conditions exist, and that they can be made
valuable by correct application there is no
doubt.

doubt. Every affair of life is preceded by
certain signs, and "coming events cast their
shadows before" in the stock market as well as
in other affairs. But these appearances should
be made use of as valuable adjuncts to more
solidly formed opinions; as a confirmation of
judgment more tangibly adduced, or as warn-
ings of possible danger.

Care has been taken to present nothing in
these pages which cannot be analyzed and explained, and while the statements made are
confirmed by both logic and precedent, they
may be easily contorted or abused.

VII

Tips

THE tip may be briefly described as illogical.

In considering this statement the dividing line between tips and information must be clearly drawn, for one is frequently found masquerading in the habit of the other.

The difference may be acceptably defined by saying that a tip is a statement that certain market movements will occur, with no accompanying reason for such movement, and that information points to the expectation of movements, founded on demonstrable probabilities.

"Smith says to buy steel," is a tip; "Smith says that the price of steel is low and that earnings are increasing," is more or less informative. In one case Smith is taken on faith and in the other his statement is open to investigation and confirmation.

The illogical character of tips will at once be apparent to the student of technical conditions. The large operator who contemplates a manipulated movement of any importance, even if such movement be based on sound reasoning, jeopardizes his own chances of success by creating a public following. This fact is so well recognized by large operators, that where a projected deal is discovered by too many people or where inside intentions have leaked in the form of a tip, they frequently abandon their plans entirely or temporarily. This point has already been discussed under the head of Technicalities, but is here reiterated as being pertinent to the subject.

The promoter of a certain speculative movement who takes the public into his confidence, is therefore either foolhardy or insincere, and the ordinary man who receives a tip may be sure his knowledge is public property. If he has good reasons for believing to the contrary and that he is the recipient of valuable and circumscribed information, his action of course depends largely on his confidence in his patron's ability to perform what is promised. He simply acts on the principle that the capacity of his informant is superior to his own, and that his integrity is unquestioned.

There are no doubt cases where manipulators have put into circulation a whispered word which they were confident would travel and be made the basis of considerable buying at a period when they wished to sell. It is related of the late Jay Gould that when approached by the pastor of a rich and fashionable New York Tabernacle, he whispered to him that purchases of Pacific Mail were very advisable, and that he, Gould, would reimburse him from his private purse if operations in that stock resulted in loss. When the pastor came to him later, deeply distressed by his large personal loss, Mr. Gould was as good as his word and promptly handed him a check to cover the deficit. "But how about my parishioners?" inquired the reverend gentleman, "you placed no ban of secrecy upon me, and their losses are enormous." To which Mr. Gould replied calmly, "They were the people I was after."

Whether or not the story is true, it points a moral.

It may be said that it would be possible for a manipulator to create public buying in a stock of sufficient volume to advance prices materially, and to thus assist or accomplish his object. This has been done, but aside from the hazard to the manipulator himself through being in the company of an easily frightened herd, which he could not control, it must be admitted that the advance created by a certain amount of buying must be offset by the ensuing liquidation, and some one must suffer.

The individual who imagines himself astute enough to evade this danger, simply flatters himself that he is wiser than his fellows, and even if he is justified in this belief, the composite result is unchanged.

The great majority of so-called tips are, however, founded on nothing better than guesswork or pure invention. Although valueless, openly distributed and untraceable to any reliable source, they are always clothed in a garb of mystery and importance and are capable of much mischief, for there is a considerable speculative element who possess no individual ideas of importance and who will act rashly on the most ill-founded advice.

If the distribution of such advice were limited to charlatans and mountebanks the effects would be greatly reduced, but many of the recognized brokerage concerns load their private wires with just such matter for the purpose of creating business, usually beginning their messages with the statement that "we have it from a good source" and ending with a ridiculous injunction to keep it dark. This statement is not lightly made, but is founded upon proven and provable fact. The statement does not in any way reflect upon houses which give out such current gossip for what it is worth and allow the patrons to decide for themselves what is wheat and what is chaff. Even under such circumstances the dissemination of such news is capable of harm, but the distributors cannot be considered culpable. They are merely the purveyors of news unaccompanied by comment or recommendation.

The brokerage offices of the country are daily visited by people who have had their imagination inflamed, or their cupidity aroused by personal ideas or exaggerated stories of speculative possibilities. As they possess no special knowledge of speculative affairs they are soon lost in a maze of intricate figures, which not being understood, are productive of nothing but indecision and mental confusion. To this numerous class the tip at once appeals. Out of the mass of conflicting reports, technicalities and evasions, comes the terse advice, "Buy Southern Pacific." Here, at last, is something definite, and its air of being confidentially imparted, its transmission by telegraph from a distant city by a great brokerage concern, and its decided tone combine to lend it an importance which it in no way possesses. The man who wants to do something, but does not know what to do, acts upon it at once, and even the more seasoned traders who will cheerfully admit that tips are worthless, are moved by advice so unimportant.

And right here a word in regard to following the advice of so-called "leaders" in speculative shares or commodities. Of late this game of follow my leader has been more or less popular, especially in the cereals and in cotton. Sometimes the outspoken views of these self-constituted mentors are made public by published interviews or even by means of paid advertisements, in which emphatic opinions and advice are set forth.

This form of public invitation, fathered by names of more or less importance or notoriety in speculative circles, is frequently effective in creating a considerable following. A little analytical thought will adduce the fact that the individual who invokes such a following must do so for one of two reasons: either because he is ignorant of the necessary ingredient of a successful campaign or because he wishes to sell what he is inviting the public to buy. Take your choice.

Follow mentally the operation of such advice and the danger is most apparent. At the first sign of this public touting the men of weight and importance who are interested in the stock or commodity involved, far from welcoming such assistance, liquidate their holdings quietly and step aside. They may be convinced of the merits of their original venture, and may even admit that the arguments set forth by the public prophet are correct, but they also know that his advice will invariably result in the commodity recommended passing from strong into weak hands, a fact which reduces the chances of profit, and increases the danger of decline, or even panic.

The trader who believes in his speculative Daniel may see the most favorable signs for a time, but he may ponder on this fact: that however honest his prophet may be in his advice he will not publicly express himself as to a consummation or reversal of his ideas and hopes until he, himself, has liquidated.

In other words, after the aimable instructor of the people has sold to his own followers all he possesses he may bluffly and candidly state that he has sold out, and advise his friends to do likewise in a market which will not now absorb their composite holdings.

The danger in such a campaign as that illustrated above is increased just in proportion to the chief promoter's influence. Each new public follower means a worse condition of affairs, and all such campaigns have finally terminated in disaster. The leader of these "come-on-boys" affairs is always a tremendous gambler, and usually an unscrupulous one.

It goes without saying that tips are frequently more or less correct. If founded on mere guesswork, the chances of success or failure are equal. If the tip failed always or even in a large majority of cases, the evil would cure itself, but the percentage of satisfactory results is great enough to encourage its deluded followers.

So prevalent is this practice of trading on flimsy advice that a large number of concerns dignified with the title of "Information Bureaus" have recently been formed. As these concerns continue to increase in number and scope, it is the natural presumption that they find followers. These "Bureaus" make extravagant claims of inside information and advance knowledge of certain future market movements in the face of the fact that no man, great or small, knows positively the result of even one day's movement. The greatest speculator or manipulator in Wall Street may enter the arena in the morning confident of certain results, and leave it at night a ruined man.

Nevertheless, claims of accurate foreknowledge by these mountebanks find a resting place in the minds of people otherwise intelligent. It is needless to add that the tipping bureau exploits its correct guesses in glowing colors, and maintains a dignified silence on the subject of its errors.

The man who invests in such so-called "information" may save his money and obtain just as good results by basing his operations on the flipping of a coin.

The concerns criticized above are in no way to be confounded with the reliable bureaus of information, of which a few are in existence. These latter are exactly what their names suggest. They gather, compile and distribute general news on speculative matters, and are useful to the active trader in presenting to him statistical results involving considerable labor, and general news which might have been overlooked. Such bureaus do not issue tips; they may allude to the existence of a certain tip, but only as a matter of current gossip. In this regard they are no more to be criticized than the editor of a newspaper who prints the record of a murder.

So far as the efficiency of the tip is concerned as shown by precedent, it may be dismissed by again falling back on the statement that no sustained speculative successes are traceable to its use.

The tip holds no dangers for the man who knows because he has taken the trouble to find out. If it conflicts with his well-grounded opinions it is discarded as being merely an unsupported statement, and opposed to more dependable deductions. If it accords with his opinions it is of no value as it is merely a belated expression of what he already knows. To such individuals the only tangible effect of which the tip is capable is its possible stimulation to investigation.

VIII

Mechanical Speculation

A NY system or method of speculation which is founded on repetition, or which contemplates ventures founded entirely on certain prices being reached regardless of conditions or values, may best be described as mechanical.

The use of such methods is extensive, and even where no set figures or forms are employed we find the average trader continually harping on last month's or last year's low points and forming for himself a mental chart by which he is frequently induced to make commitments.

Of these numerous mechanical methods of speculation only two possess sufficient merit to warrant serious consideration. These two exceptions are the scale order and the stop loss order, both of which may be made useful under certain conditions. That these methods are frequently abused goes without saying. They are often made the sole basis of operations instead of adjuncts, in which case they fail of their purpose.

Either method is useful only as an auxiliary to sound judgments already formed. So employed they possess certain merit in that they permit of a fixed mechanical arrangement for accumulation or protection.

The contention is here submitted that the scale order should be used only for the purpose of acquiring a line of stocks at low prices, and the stop loss order for the protection of profits after an advance. Otherwise employed they become useless, and in some cases even assist in producing loss.

The intelligent use of the scale order contemplates the purchase of a certain stock or commodity at fixed intervals below the first purchase price until the total proposed purchase is completed, the mechanical principle being that an advance of one-half the decline on which the purchases are made leaves the trader without loss, and the broader general principle being that the votary of the method at all times allows for declines due to accidents or errors of judgment. If such declines occur, he gradually acquires his line at a lower average price for the whole.

As an example, embodying both these prin-

ciples, suppose that a purchase of one thousand
shares of Union Pacific common is contemplated. The scaler begins his purchases at,
say 100, taking one hundred shares at that
price and entering an order to buy one hundred
shares at fixed points below the first price, say
for instance, at 99, 98, 97, 96, 95, 94, 93, 92 and
91, at which last named price his purchase
would be completed at an average price of
95½.

The amount to be purchased on each decline, the width of the gap between declines,
and the point to which purchases are to be continued are of course matters of individual determination. The principal drawback to this
method, which is at once apparent, is the
danger of the original, or some intermediate
purchase, being made at such a low point as to
prevent the accumulation of the proposed line.
In the extreme case of only the initial purchase
having been possible, the trader finds himself
with a profit on only one hundred shares of
stock where he had intended to carry one
thousand.

But this argument against the merits of the
method may be answered as follows:

The average speculator may safely assume
that a decline from the point he considers low

is probable. If he happens to catch the low price it is an accident and not because of his method, whose virtues must be reserved for future usefulness. He may congratulate himself on an unusually fortunate purchase and be satisfied with his comparatively small but quickly acquired gains. A profit is a profit, and the market is always with him. On the other hand, if he is so good a judge of the market that his purchase was a result of judgment rather than accident, he has no use for the scale order or any other such assistance.

The scale order is frequently misused by depending too much upon inherent virtues which it does not possess. That is to say, it is made the basis of operations which are indulged in more on a belief in the merits of the method than on any intelligently formed opinion of the probable action of the stock, or a sufficient consideration of actual value, technical conditions, etc. The probabilities of an advance equal to half the preceding decline is upheld by precedent and makes the method alluring, but granting such an advance, and no more, nothing has been gained when it materializes.

In short, it may be said that the scale order used as a basis for poor purchases is generally useless. So employed it differs from ordinary methods only in the fact that it will take the trader a little longer to lose his money.

But he who admits that natural market action, manipulation or accident render it improbable that even a careful study of his intended venture will find for him the lowest price and who wishes to adopt a methodical plan of operation—for him the scale order presents some very favorable features, and is recommended for serious consideration.

The study of precedent will show that the scaling method could have been successfully employed in almost every standard listed security. In fact precedent will show entirely too much, in that it presents the fact that the method carried out indefinitely would seldom have resulted in loss from any point, high or low. Even taking the worst possible example, a stock so greatly inflated and so widely discredited as Amalgamated Copper, scaling from its extreme high price of 130 in 1901 to the extreme low price of 33⅝ in 1903 would give an average price of 82, a point recently exceeded in market prices.

But such figuring as this is useless. An extended campaign of this kind contemplates the use of a vast sum of money, always available in cash.

The danger of pursuing statistics so alluring as those presented by a study of past market movements as applied to the scaling process lies in pointing to what money can do rather than what it should do, and in indulging in mental and statistical proofs, the actual operations of which are past the possibilities of the purse. Even if the financial equation is granted, few men possess the stability, patience and courage to adhere to the rules of such an extended and unsatisfying campaign, and without such adherence the whole structure falls to the ground.

The best use that can be made of the scale order is, therefore, to use it only for the methodical making of purchases already deemed advisable. If the first purchase by this method is made at the point at which prior investigation and judgment has pointed out as the time to buy, irrespective of any inherent virtues which may lie in the scaling process, it can seldom result in injury, and will generally prove beneficial. If the method is adopted it must be adhered to rigidly, unless for some good reason the deal is abandoned entirely. In the majority of cases this is not done, the operator for some reason, impatience, greed, or fright, changing his plans, in which case the usefulness of the method is impaired or eliminated.

The stop loss order is one of the most abused of the methods employed by traders, for, like the scale order, it is frequently used at the wrong periods, or given credit for too much inherent virtue.

In speaking of this method, no reference is made to the stop order as employed by brokers for self-protection, in which case it is a matter of necessity. The point to be considered is its value when used voluntarily by the trader for his own benefit.

There is an axiom among traders that the best principle in speculation is to take small losses and large profits. So popular is this axiom that many speculators consider it the great secret of success, and in following it employ the stop loss order continually in a most haphazard manner.

The expressed theory of small losses and large gains sounds good and is all very well in itself, but it may be relegated entirely to a class who wish to gamble on quotations on a reversal of ordinary public methods, which is to take large losses and small profits. The small loss trader pins his faith wholly to the belief that a market will swing not to, but past the point where he placed his stop loss.

On this theory all intelligent figuring as to the probable future movements is eliminated, and the success is based wholly on mechanical chance, in which case the probability of loss and gain is exactly the same; that is to say, the probability of ten losses of one point each, or one gain of ten points, is the same. Those who combat the truth of this statement at once array themselves as opposed to the expressed and accepted consensus of opinion of the world's greatest students of the doctrine of mathematical chance.

To contend that any element of intelligent forecast of market movement could be combined with the use of the small loss theory as outlined above, is untenable, for if a purchase is made because research has shown such purchase warranted by conditions and the price of the stock, we find the stop loss trader in the ridiculous position of selling his holdings below a price he first considered should be cheap, at which point he should in reality be contemplating further purchases.

So rooted in some minds is the principle of small loss and large gain, that an attack on the virtues of such a proceeding will no doubt be bitterly contested. The argument against it however, is sound; it is purely mechanical, cannot be combined with intelligent operations, has no marked success to its credit, and is not adopted by successful traders, i. e. those who buy because they consider a thing too low, and sell because they consider it too high.

But there are certain periods when the use of a fixed limitation of decline is entitled to consideration. The trader may find himself in possession of certain profits in a market which is high, but which his judgment tells him may, for technical or other reasons, still advance materially. At such a period he may wish to provide against accident, or a vicious raid by placing stop loss orders below his holdings at a point which will insure him the bulk of his profit, advancing the point at which loss shall be stopped as the market advances.

Taken the year round, the chance of loss or profit from such a course is, as has been stated, demonstrably equal; but in the case of high prices, the extraneous dangers of accident or manipulation, and the advisability of protecting profits by systematic orders contemplating such dangers, the placing of stop orders is frequently useful. Even at such periods its principal virtue lies in the pre-arrangement of a desirable course which might be disturbed by mental confusion or personal absence.

It is a debatable question whether it would not be better to buy when conditions and prices show that purchases are warranted, and, per contra, to liquidate when danger threatens or when prices look high enough. But to most traders systematic arrangement is desirable, and to some minds absolutely necessary.

As recommended above, the scale order and stop loss order in no way interfere with the workings of study and judgment, and are frequently employed by traders whose opinions are entitled to respect. Let the fact be taken to heart however, that employed as a means of speculation, rather than as an aid to it, neither method possesses any merit whatever.

" Chart System "

There is an incredibly large number of traders who pin their faith to the so-called "chart system" of speculation, which recommends the study of past movements and prices, and bases operations thereon. So popular is this plan that concerns which make a business of preparing and issuing such charts do a thriving business.

The theory propounded is that history repeats itself, and that because a property sold at a certain low price on some previous occasion and then advanced, the same thing will occur again! There are various offshoots and modifications of the system, but the basic plan is founded wholly on repetition, regardless of actual conditions. The idea is absolutely fatuous, entirely untrustworthy, and highly dangerous. The study of the past is interesting and instructive in showing what may be expected in the way of general movements, but when we are asked to throw reason and research to one side in favor of only half-demonstrated repetitions, the theory becomes untenable.

The chart traders would have us pore over musty records of past movements, and have us buy a stock at a certain price because it sold there before, without stopping even to investigate the fact that conditions in that particular stock have changed materially. The votary of this plan might find himself cheerfully buying the shares of a bankrupt and ruined corporation in its very process of financial disintegration, or on the other hand might refrain from purchases at very low prices because it sold at still lower prices on some previous occasion.

Another class of retrospective speculators base their operations on seasons, or even corresponding weeks and months, forming their opinions on insufficient research, or on nothing at all. If there were in truth any certain period of the year or month from which movements would occur, the whole world would know it, and such knowledge would reverse expectations by the rotten technical conditions it would create.

It is useless to enlarge upon the various methods employed by the mechanical traders, for they are all alike in that they resolve the whole speculative structure into a gambling machine, with a large percentage against the player. To the large number of people who risk their money in this manner, and who contend that there is no use in trying to accurately forecast probable movements by actual investigation, let the following statement be made:

The man who buys a stock at fifty dollars a share because he has good reasons for believing that it is worth one hundred dollars, or who sells at one hundred dollars on account of having good reasons for believing it worth only fifty dollars, is the only man in the speculative world who succeeds.

When the study and thought necessary to

forming such conclusions intelligently are eliminated in favor of any or all other methods, the colossal error is made of expurging from the plan of operations the only possible chance of sustained success, the great basic principle to which all other knowledge, technical or statistical, is purely subsidiary.

IX

Short Selling

THE practice of short selling, which was formerly largely confined to the professional element, has of late years become quite fashionable among those members of the trading public who speculate regularly, and has been even more disastrous than have ventures for the long accounts.

The basis for this action, and the growing popularity of the short side is founded on natural pig-headed pessimism which will listen to no argument, and is incapable of clear reasoning; or what is more common, on contentions so shallow and silly that it seems superfluous to record them on a printed page.

Everywhere one hears the belief expressed that the "big money" is made on the short side, and that the greatest inside speculators are Bears. This view is entirely erroneous.

One of the favorite arguments of the public bear element is as follows: the public generally buys, and the public generally loses money.

Therefore the buying side is the losing side and the short side is the winning side. By this absurd and wholly unfounded deduction many bears are created.

Now, the fact of the matter is that the fortunes made on the short side of stocks are few and far between, while those accumulated by judicious operations on the long side are legion. The public loses its money, not because it purchases, but because its purchases are made at the wrong periods and its methods of operation are bad.

The accumulated wealth of the Vanderbilts, Rockefellers, Astors and Goulds has accrued from the continued increase in the valuation of properties in which they were interested. True, all these lights of finance have been justly accused at times of operating for lower prices. This is particularly true of the late Jay Gould, who was widely known as a wrecker. But the wrecking operations were solely for the purpose of driving other holders out of a certain corporation and creating a sentiment and condition which would permit of the purchase of a controlling interest in the corporation in question at low prices.

So few have been the individuals who operated on the short side habitually and success-

fully that the names of Travers and Cammack
stand out in bold relief among the horde of
great traders, and the operations of the successful minority were carefully calculated as
to periods and safety. Their skillful work and
clear foresight would probably have made
more money for them if their operations had
been reversely conducted.

"It took me ten years, and cost me two fortunes to become an optimist, but it was worth
all it cost," said a successful speculator of today, and in that terse sentence is much food
for thought. It is possible to make money on
the short side of the market, but it is very difficult, and the man who is capable of acting
with enough judgment and decision to accumu-
late gains working against the current is
doubly capable of succeeding by swimming
with it.

The semi-professional traders who trade on
the short side, as a rule, exercise no more
judgment or study of actual valuation than do
the army who purchase. They are moved by
blue talk and general pessimism, and sell at
the bottom and are frightened out at the top.
Their operations are simply bad in inverse
ratio. There is one difference: the purchaser
who has the means and patience to stand by an

ill-timed purchase will eventually see daylight, while there is no certainty of this desirable consummation for the bear. On the other hand, he may see his venture grow more and more disastrous as time and the advance of the country increases the value of the stock he has sold. The cycles of speculation will of course bring him occasional hope, but these cycles occurring from a gradually ascending pivotal point carry him further from his original price at each revolution.

The short seller of stocks has against him at all times the natural future enhancement of values, and more specifically, the earnings and dividends of the securities in which he trades.

To make this more clear let us say that one hundred shares of a certain stock, paying 6%, are sold short at par, its normal price, and the commitment endures for one year. For the sake of argument all speculative movements will be eliminated, and the assumption made that at the end of the year the selling price of the stock is still par. It will be seen that the seller has had his account charged with six hundred dollars in dividends, and thus while there has been no advance in the posted value of his stock, he has lost six hundred dollars.

This does not hold good in the case of a purchase, for even if the high rate of 6% is paid on the unmargined balance, these charges are covered by the dividends credited to the stock, and the normal gain of 6% has been made on the actual money deposited as margin.

For example: one hundred shares of a 6% stock purchased at par on ten points margin, and sold at the same price one year later, shows as follows:

Total purchase price of stock.........$10,000
Marginal deposit..................... 1,000

Unpaid balance...................... $9,000
Int. for 1 yr. at 6% on unpaid bal.$540
Credit account dividends........ 600

Credit balance.................. $60

Or 6% on the thousand dollars actually involved.

And on the other hand:

One hundred shares of the same stock sold at par and re-purchased at the same price one year later:

Total credit from sale of stock.......$10,000
Total debit from purchase......$10,000
Debit for one year's dividends..   600

A loss of $600. If it is presumed that one

thousand dollars has been deposited as margins, on which amount an allowance of 6% has been made by the broker, there is still a net deficit of $540, with no adverse market action.

In the above examples no account is taken of commission charges, but the exhibit is in no wise affected by this omission, as the commission charges on the short side would increase the loss on that commitment exactly as much as it decreases the gain on the purchase.

It will be seen, therefore, that the short seller has working against him at all times a tangible effect capable of exact demonstration. The contention is sometimes made that short commitments are seldom carried for any considerable period, and that the man who sells short today and re-purchases tomorrow, escapes this onus. This view is so shallow that it is unnecessary to state to thinking men that the difference is wholly a matter of degree, and that the Bear in dividend paying shares swims constantly against the current.

What is true of one year is equally true of one day, and repeated short time operations multiply the infinitesimal drawback until it is as great as when lumped on one longer contract.

And the seller of non-dividend paying stocks is no better off, for he combats either the earnings which are accruing, or the gradual enhancement of the stock through a wise distribution of these earnings. In short, whether a habitual short seller sells dividend or non-dividend paying shares he tampers continually with progress. He makes his venture on the side of disaster, accident, dishonesty, mismanagement, and pessimism, rather than on the side of gradual improvement in the business affairs and conditions of the country.

Another pitfall which besets the short seller is the danger of deliberate cornering, or of a fight for control in his stock. Tremendous advances are possible in either case, and even if his sales have been made at high prices he faces this hazard. The plea that such great twists are infrequent will not do, for to be overtaken by one such squeeze in a decade is sufficient to wipe out a great portion, or all, of the accumulated gains of that period.

Concentration of wealth and power make such upward manipulation more possible from day to day, and this latter statement develops another argument, and another important fact in answer to that argument.

The argument is simply that history shows

that severe breaks, and drives against certain stocks have been made more frequently than corners or squeezes. Drives have been made against a certain stock which in a few days carried that stock to ridiculously low figures, and later it was re-purchased by the same interest which wrought the havoc in values.

This is admitted—as a record of the past. Such action is out of the question today. The method is pursued to some extent, but great declines in a brief period no longer come from savage individual attacks on certain securities. The reason for this is simple; the concentration of capital mentioned above, makes such action too hazardous. There was a time when Mr. Keene would, for a single great interest, pound the price of Sugar off twenty, thirty, or forty points in a day or two, and then re-purchase it at low figures. Mr. Keene will never do it again, for the enormous sales necessary to accomplish this coup would place him and his sponsors in danger of losing control of the stock. There are now other powerful interests well enough aware of the value of Sugar stock which would welcome any opportunity of wresting the control from present hands, and if the well-named manipulator were to do today what he did even a decade ago, he would wake up some morning not only minus the control of the property, but opposed, in a market sense, to interests even more powerful than those he represented.

This places the moneyed speculative interests in the position of allowing public folly, rather than individual efforts, to bring about great declines and low prices, under which condition the danger of losing control is a matter of vigilance and a matching of wits, or possibly a community of interests against this same public.

There is no gainsaying the fact that it is possible to so accurately judge of values and periods as to make money on both sides of a market cycle, but those who have been successful in so doing may be numbered on the fingers.

The frequently quoted aphorism of a great latter day speculator: "If it's a good sale at all it's a good short sale," meaning that if one is justified in selling holdings to realize profits, he is also justified in selling short, will not bear the light of calm analysis.

There is a vast difference between accepting accumulated profits, and being absolutely free from further risk with an acquired gain in bank, and being in a position to lose heavily through market action.

In view of the above facts it would appear that for the speculator in the ordinary walks of life, the safest course is to confine operations to purchases of stocks when they are cheap, and to limit sales to the realizing of profits. This course necessitates periods of non-participation which are decidedly beneficial. It permits the operator to look with an unprejudiced eye upon market actions, frees him of a direct percentage working against him in dividends and earnings, and best of all, maps out for him a fixed and settled plan of operations, conducted with the current of irresistible improvement and certain accretion.

X

What 500 Speculative Accounts Showed

A N examination of almost four thousand speculative accounts, extending over a period of ten years, developed results interesting and instructive in many ways. The examination was of an exhaustive character, and covered operations of every conceivable nature in both stocks and cereals.

In these accounts all the errors of speculation were distinctly illustrated.

The three principal points developed by the investigation were that 80% of the accounts showed a final loss; that the tendency to buy at the top and sell at the bottom was most prevalent; and that most of the operations appeared to be of a purely gambling character. The further fact was established that success almost invariably led to excesses.

The mass of figures derived from so extensive an examination being voluminous and complicated, it was considered advisable to simplify the matter for presentation in this work, pursuant to which decision, the following plan was hit upon.

It was decided to use for illustration a single stock, trading in which predominated in the operations covering a certain period. In order that the illustration should be perfectly fair it was decided to make the period begin and end with the stock considered, selling at the same approximate price.

As U. S. Steel Common offered the best illustration, 500 accounts, either confined to operations in this stock, or showing a large percentage of deals in that security, were selected. The period originally contemplated was from January to December of the year 1901, but was discarded on the theory that the results shown would be abnormal, owing to the panic of May ninth of that year. It might be contended that the tremendous losses sustained in this panic were offset by the unusual opportunities for purchases at low prices, but as few purchases were shown it was thought best to seek a period during which nothing abnormal occurred, but which presented numerous advances and declines of an ordinary character.

Such a condition existed from July, 1901, to March, 1903, during which time there were numerous advances and declines in Steel Common ranging between 29¾ and 46¾. In July, 1901, the stock sold at 37, and in March, 1903, it touched the same price, and as the price at the beginning and ending of the period is the same, and furthermore is nearly midway between highest and lowest prices, it would appear that about equal chances had been presented for profit or loss if the element of knowledge and mental acumen were cancelled.

In other words, viewed wholly as a gambling proposition the chances, not considering the percentage of commissions, were about equal. The reason for making this comparison will be apparent later.

The books of the different firms showed a marked unanimity of public action at all times, reflecting a general consensus of opinion. This applied not only to the 500 accounts chosen for this illustration, but to all which were originally examined.

In selecting these 500 accounts every precaution was taken to exercise absolute fairness. No picking over was indulged in, as it is obvious that the balance of gain or loss might be thrown materially to one side or the other by such a process. In order to prove the total result as compared with the whole, the loss on the entire number of shares handled in the 500 accounts was compared with the loss on the total number of shares in the entire four thousand accounts, (operations in grain and other commodities not being considered), and the result was found to be harmonious.

No preconceived ideas nor prejudices were permitted to enter the investigation, the object sought being to establish figures which might be considered fairly indicative of what usually occurred in public speculative affairs under normal conditions.

It will be understood that the facts and figures hereafter presented were based wholly upon total results, the entire number of accounts being finally viewed in a composite light. On this theory the following results were discovered:

Three hundred and forty-three accounts resulted in a net loss at their termination; 88 accounts resulted in a net profit; 52 accounts were even or showed inconsiderable differences. The result of 17 accounts is unknown, as the Steel stocks represented were taken up by the purchasers, in all cases at a considerable paper loss.

The total deficit on all losing accounts was.....................$1,245,000
The total gain on all profitable accounts 288,000

Leaving a net deficit of........... $957,000

The total number of shares handled was
1,112,000, of which 820,000 shares were originally purchases, and 292,000 originally short
sales.

The total brokerage charges, commissions,
interest, etc., were $275,000, which amount is
included in the total loss.

The comparative losses on short sales, share
for share, were about 20% greater than the
losses on purchases.

The favorite method of operation was to
purchase or sell on slight reactions from high
or low prices.

The average price of all purchases for long
account was 42⅝, and the average price of all
short sales was 35¾.

The scale order was employed in 53 accounts, (42 long and 11 short), but was either
abandoned or interfered with in all but eight
instances.

There were numerous evidences of systems
being used; this is not susceptible of proof, but

the uniform character of the trading as shown by constant repetitions was considered good evidence of a fixed method. Over 90% of the accounts of this description resulted in loss.

In 23 instances an inverted scale order was employed, purchases being made at fixed intervals as the stock advanced. This is the principle called "going with the market." It failed in every instance.

In considering the above figures, the first and most vital point is the predominance of loss over profit under conditions as nearly equal as possible to present. The reason for considering the matter in the light of a gambling transaction was to develop the fact that the total loss was distinctly greater than the percentage against the trader as represented by commissions, the loss being $957,000, and the commission charges only $275,000.

As the price of the stock at the beginning and end of the period considered was the same, and as nothing of an abnormal character occurred, this additional loss must be attributed to other causes, and here the mechanical drawback ends and the personal equation enters.

Everything being equal, the surplus loss of $682,000 must be attributed to erroneous mental operations, and when the further fact is considered that the average price paid for stocks was 42⅝, and the average price at which stocks were sold was 35¾, the theory that the public reverses the methods dictated by reason is confirmed. It is apparent that if this proclivity had not been indulged in the result would have been a net profit; that is to say, if 37 had been taken as a pivotal point, and purchases made below, or sales above it, numerous gains could have been made on either side, especially on purchases, as the short seller would have had about 6 points in dividends against him during the period, which has not been considered in the figures given, but which is reflected with considerable accuracy in the composite result.

An examination of financial columns and current gossip at corresponding periods of high and low prices showed no well founded reasons for the consensus of opinion at such times.

The gossip rather reflected than incited the prevailing cheerful or pessimistic feeling, and no particular mischief can be attributed to this source.

Next in importance to the suicidal tendency to sell cheap and buy dear was the widespread evidence of greed. In almost every case where an account was successfully begun, the operations were immediately extended in volume until, even after a large number of successful results, a single reverse wiped out the entire credit. Even those operators who showed apparent good judgment in buying and selling were subject to this fault to so marked a degree that after being right nine times and wrong once, they were on the debit side of the ledger.

The inability of the average trader to map out a plan and follow it was also distinctly exemplified. Methods and systems begun and pursued for a time with mathematical precision almost invariably ended in a mass of indiscriminate operations caused apparently by fright or confusion in case of loss, and exhilaration and enthusiasm if successful.

Another interesting development was that the accounts of those speculators who operated from a distance, or from points where no brokerage office was located, made a better showing than those of local traders. The losses were smaller and the gains larger. The contrast was so marked that it would appear that isolation has its advantages. The marginal provision made by these distant traders was more ample, and the operations were fewer in number. These two points alone were a decided advantage. They also escaped the ill-advised action frequently induced by flurries and canards, and altogether seemed to operate more intelligently, possibly because the opportunities to make fools of themselves were restricted.

In considering the above figures and deductions, it must be constantly borne in mind that the market covered a comparatively narrow range for an active stock; that no unusual opportunities for profit or loss existed, and that the end of the period showed the stock unchanged in price.

In comparing it with a great cycle of speculative prices the results would be greatly magnified. The object in view was to submit results entirely of a normal nature.

It is doubtful whether operations in U. S. Steel stock were particularly desirable at any time during the period mentioned, as it presented no great immediate promise, and numerous dangers at all times. There were many surface indications of a warning character. The stock was untried; the earnings were comparatively so large as to suggest inflation, and the fact of it being a public favorite was proof of a bad technical condition.

The student of the technical position of shares would have reasoned that the enormous

floating supply of the stock in public speculative hands would make any marked or sustained advance impossible, as any considerable
appreciation in the market price would meet
with enough selling to stop the upward trend,
while the danger of panic or severe decline
would be increased for exactly the same reasons.

It is therefore probable that the better class of
traders shunned the stock entirely, especially
when the fact is considered that numerous
other active stocks presented better opportunities during the period considered.

For instance, Louisville & Nashville made
and maintained an advance of $25 per share
from July, 1901, to March, 1903, the advance
being justified by improved conditions in the
South.

Nevertheless U. S. Steel was the public
favorite, and was obviously the best example
of public speculation.

Viewed in the light of comparative results,
the loss of $682,000 on total transactions of
1,112,000 shares may at first blush be considered small, only a little over fifty cents per
share, but it must be remembered that this was
a total deficit on all operations, and that the
numerous profits made at various times were

used as an offset to losses. The question is, why should any loss have occurred when there was no decline in market valuation?

If the barometrical character of the examination outlined above is admitted, the fact is established that a loss was sustained which can be attributed to nothing but mistaken methods and impulses. In other words, the actual percentage against the trader was more than trebled by personal actions, a thing which would not have been possible with any mechanical gambling device.

The matter presented in this chapter offers much food for thought. It is not in line with the alluring view of speculative opportunities frequently presented to the public eye. The statements already made that speculation could be made profitable, are in no way modified, but the disease must be diagnosed before it can be treated, and some of the medicine necessary to financial health has a bitter taste.

Written large between the lines of every disastrous speculative account are the reasons for failure. True, this is cold comfort, for the losses represented cannot be recovered by analysis, but the lesson may be of great value in its bearing on future ventures.

Discovering and charting submerged and

dangerous rocks by a process of shipwrecking is an unpleasant method of acquiring knowledge, but a most forcible one.

XI

Grain Speculation

AS a confirmation of the preconceived theory that the percentage of loss in grain speculation was much greater than in stocks, an examination of accounts was undertaken based on the same general lines outlined in stocks.

The commodity chosen for investigation was No. 2 Wheat, and the transactions considered were made on prices established on the Chicago Board of Trade.

The period covered was from January, 1901, at which time the price was 76⅜, to December, 1903, when the price was 77¾.

During this period of three years the lowest price touched was 63⅛ in July, 1901, and the highest price, 95 in September, 1902.

The range for each of the three years was:

63½ to 79½ in 1901.

67½ to 95 in 1902.

70¼ to 93 in 1903.

These figures are presented as evidence of

numerous wide speculative movements occurring between the same comparative basic prices at the beginning and ending of the three years.

Five hundred accounts were found available for dissection, and the same appearance of unanimity of operations as that apparent in stocks was shown.

The principal seeming difference between stock and grain trading was that the public indulged more freely in operations for the short account in grain than in stocks. Several instances were discovered where for a time the preponderance of operations were for short account, invariably at low prices and on the eve of an advance.

All the errors illustrated in stocks were found to exist in grain on a magnified scale. The tendency to buy at the top, and sell at the bottom, was particularly marked, and while the average buying price of 79⅛ may look low, it may be said in explanation that the prices of 95c. in 1902, and 93c. in 1903, were of a manipulated nature, and of very brief duration, and that comparatively few transactions were possible at very high prices. If these two abnormal periods are eliminated, the average price was high.

The investigation resulted as follows:

412 accounts showed a final loss.

74 accounts showed a final profit.

14 accounts were neutral.

The total deficit on all losing accounts was $923,000. The total gain on all profitable accounts, $52,000, leaving a net deficit of $871,000.

The total amount of grain handled was 90,000,000 bushels (the speculative equivalent of 900,000 shares of stock), of which 62,000,000 bushels were originally purchases, and 28,000,000 originally short sales.

The total brokerage charges were $112,500.

The comparative losses on short sales were 16% less than on purchases.

The scale order was employed in 140 accounts, (92 long and 48 short), but was pursued to an uninterrupted conclusion in only 21 instances.

The average buying price was 79⅛, and the average selling price 70⅜.

The principal facts illustrated as compared with stock operations are a net loss of $757,000 over and above an actual mechanical percentage of only $112,500, and the small total of gross profits as compared with the total of gross losses.

It has been stated that the grain investigation was begun with the preconceived opinion that losses in grain would be proportionately larger than those in stocks, and the result, as far as it goes, is confirmatory. It is only fair to state in this respect that losses shown in corn were comparatively larger than in stocks, but much smaller than in wheat. This is probably explained by the fact that corn has undergone a readjustment of valuation through its increased uses, and enormous increase of exportation, both of the cereal itself and its by-products, and also the fact that we raise 80% of the world's corn, and that available acreage is about exhausted.

These facts were so patent as to be of assistance to even the obtuse mind of the ordinary speculator, and as purchases predominated, and the price has gradually advanced, comparative losses were smaller.

The preconceived opinion as to losses in grain operations was based upon the irrefutable fact that study and judgment must in such operations be largely superseded by purely gambling principles. In other words, the probable price of grain cannot be intelligently forecasted by the ordinary speculator, as no reliable figures are obtainable, and no prophecies as to future conditions can be reliably adduced. The annual crop scares are not dependable, and actual conditions which bear upon future prices are available only to the chosen few who can afford to make their own expensive investigations!

It is needless to say that possessors of valuable knowledge do not diffuse their information, nor expose their operations to public view until the psychological moment arrives at which they wish to sell.

It is possible to obtain figures as to the earnings of corporations, and such figures being at hand, the rest is a matter of judgment and study, but no figures which may be considered a safe basis of operations are obtainable anent cereals.

In addition to the gambling elements which this lack of knowledge injects into operations in cereals, they are much more subject to manipulation. The record of a single individual "dumping" the entire speculative public in wheat, is not rare in the history of grain speculation, and the capital employed in the operation would not make a hearty meal for Wall Street.

There is another drawback to grain speculation as compared with stocks, and while it is apparently overlooked or ignored by the average trader, it is important, and is as follows:

The possessor of 100 shares of stock bought at a normal price, is the recipient of dividends, or may naturally expect ultimate improvement in his security if it is a good one.

The possessor of 10,000 bushels of grain at a normal price is subject to storage charges and insurance, and has equal chances of profit or loss in future prices.

To illustrate this: The man who invests $10,-000 in a 6% stock, at par, receives $600 per year on his investment, while he who invests the same amount in 10,000 bushels of wheat at $1.00 per bushel, pays about $1,200 a year to carry his property. This is looking at the matter as a cash proposition, but the comparative drawback cannot be escaped by any form of operations for the long account, whether the transaction be for one day or one year.

The optional nature of grain presents another drawback in that an unfortunate operation cannot be continued indefinitely, except by the process of transferring to more deferred options with a multiplication of commission charges. Even by this process the transferred trade may be regarded in the light of a new transaction, as the buyer's original reasons for believing that the present, or coming crop, would be salable at a certain price before the maturity of the option purchased, have been entirely obliterated by the lapse of time, and he now finds himself depending upon the chances of recovering in the new transaction the losses sustained in the old.

If he accepts and pays for the commodity, and a year later finds that the price has advanced 12 cents, his position is in no way improved, as the expense of carrying his product for that period has offset the higher market value.

The trader who purchases wheat has against him, therefore, all the ordinary drawbacks of misleading appearances, manipulation, etc., but in addition, the element of purely gambling chance is greatly increased, and a tremendous submerged percentage added.

The foregoing statements at once suggest the question, "If successful operations for the long account are so difficult, why should not operations on the other side present advantages in direct inverse ratio?"

The point is well taken, and the answer is simply, "they do present such opportunities." This advantage is illustrated to some extent by the fact that operations for the short account, in grain, showed a larger ratio of profit, or rather, a smaller ratio of loss, than was found in purchases.

But in public short selling we find that a too general recognition of its advantages would lead to the undoing of the trader by creating a technical position which would be very inviting to the moneyed manipulators. This danger must be considered, as well as the fact that the theory of accidents being in favor of the short seller of stocks, is exactly reversed in grain. For instance, war, classed as the greatest of all calamities under certain conditions, is an invariable reason for higher prices in food products. The tendency to sell at low prices also prevails and must be overcome if operations for the short account are to prove profitable; but brushing aside all these elements of accident or error, it may be stated that the short seller of cereals possesses a distinct advantage.

The fact will no doubt be pointed out that short operations have proved uniformly disastrous in the past few years. While this is granted, it in no way interferes with the arguments but rather supports them in its demonstration of the possibilities of manipulation by

one or two individuals. But there is another
reason for this reversal of form which was
apparently recognized by a few men and stub-
bornly overlooked by the majority. The fact
is that all staples have recently undergone a
process of revaluation to a higher basis and
that the seller of every product has worked
against the current of this universal readjustment.

That the public is slow to recognize changed
conditions is demonstrated by the fact that
the period of high prices from the latter part
of 1888 to early in 1892 finally educated them
to consider one dollar the normal price of
wheat at just the time when a readjustment to
lower valuation took place and enormous
losses were sustained by a tenacious adherence
to this theory of dollar wheat until the expensive lesson had been ground into them that a
change had occurred. The more recent readjustment to high prices was likewise un-
recognized and vigorously combatted.

This is a very marked evidence of the fact
that speculators generally move more on a
mental chart of recent market action than upon
any broad lines of thought.

It would be really amusing to review the
opportunities set forth by the advocates of the

so-called chart system as applied to grain trading for the last fifteen years. We find them in the position of purchasing wheat through a period of depression and later selling it persistently through a period of advancing prices, for it must be admitted that changed conditions cannot be contemplated in a fixed system founded on past, not future events. The votaries of the charts will no doubt attempt to evade this statement by demonstrations covering an insufficient period or by claiming that changed conditions were recognized and their little machines readjusted to meet them. The first refutation is simply unfair, and if the second is true, correct recognition would have been sufficient without any auxiliary machinery.

The difficulty of successful operations in cereals by ordinary traders is very pertinently shown by the remarks made by the most successful bucket shop man in the United States.

"I can better afford to trade flat in grain than to trade in stocks at one quarter commission; they have nothing to go on.'"

This is the statement of a man who looked upon the matter in a purely gambling light and admitted that he could eliminate the actual percentage in grain transactions and depend wholly upon the speculator beating himself.

Even the greater lights of speculation, fortified by large capital, have found the hazards of grain speculation so great, and the most careful forecasts so unreliable, that in many instances, and after disastrous experiments, they have transferred their operations wholly to stocks. Mr. James R. Keene twice retired from the Chicago arena a badly whipped man, and it is related of him that he refused an intimate friend financial assistance in a grain deal with the terse remark that he would be doing him no kindness, as it was impossible to win.

This is, of course, an extreme view, for money lost by one man must necessarily be gained by another; but this fact does not interfere with the broad general principle that stocks of good corporations are productive, and that the possession of staples is an expense. One is for perpetual existence and natural enhancement, the other for consumption.

The contention of Mr. Keene that it is impossible to make money in cereal speculation cannot be wholly concurred with. The man who is astute enough to foresee a final readjustment of values or who purchases staples at an extremely low price in periods of depression, and vice versa, will succeed; but the average grain trader will find his opportunities and possibilities reduced, and his obstacles multiplied by comparison with operations in stocks.

XII

Suggestions as to Intelligent Methods

IN deciding what to buy and when to buy it, the speculator faces the most formidable of his problems, for upon his decision upon these two points rests success or failure.

It will be necessary for him to concentrate upon this task research, labor and clear thinking, coupled with technical knowledge and sustained by precedent.

In approaching the first phase of the question—What to buy—it may be well to employ the time-honored method of elimination, and to consider primarily what not to buy.

It seems incredible that the numerous oil, mining, and other companies which advertise large returns on low priced stocks, or immense values for small investments, should find a market, but the fact remains that the money annually invested (?) in this class of stocks is so considerable an amount as to demand some comment, and warrant a note of warning.

This class of so-called securities may be

said, by and large, to have no value at all. Securities which have an actual dividend earning power of any probable duration do not go begging long in this day and age, and are seldom advertised for sale in the newspapers.

Let this fact be remembered: a mine, an oil well, or any other producing company with a demonstrable value can command a market price at all times. That is to say, if the owner, or owners of a mine can show a certain amount of ore in sight, or can prove that such ore exists, they can command a fair price for that ore as surely as if the commodity were flour in a storehouse instead of gold, silver, or copper in a mine. Any man who has a knowledge of mining affairs, (and who has no mining stock for sale), will confirm this statement.

If, therefore, the sellers of stock in such companies have a property, capable of producing a certain commodity which may be sold at a profit, they must, in order to reap any substantial benefit from the "stocking" operation, sell as much of the stock at high prices as to cover the great expense of time, a costly advertising campaign, officers' salaries, a large commission to fiscal agents, (usually 20%), and leave a margin of profit for themselves. They must, in short, sell to the public at about double the value placed on the property by men of wisdom and experience.

There are no doubt cases where the promoters of such securities believe that the value of their own property is greater than any appraised market, in which case we find their judgment opposed to that of shrewd men seeking to invest capital. In such opposition of judgment the owners may be right—the chances are a hundred to one that they are wrong.

But even the above examples are too broad, for the great majority of these concerns have no property of any demonstrable value whatever. Their stocks are made, like Hodge's razors, to sell. The promoters depend upon golden promises, statements misleading, or actually false, and public gullibility to create a market for their stocks. That they are able to sell them at all is remarkable.

These companies use every means for deceiving the public. They employ the best of writers to get up glowing prospectuses, and not infrequently the names of prominent men are found among their officials or directors. These latter individuals participate sometimes through ignorance and enthusiasm, sometimes through actual dishonesty. In either case it may be justly stated that a prominent name added to the roster of an advertising company is not sufficient proof of the property's merit.

In addition to these facts there is no recognized market for this class of stocks, and they cannot be disposed of like listed securities, at a moment's notice. This is in itself a great drawback.

In making these statements there is no prejudice nor desire to be unfair. There are no doubt exceptions to the rule, but these exceptions are so rare that the best plan possible is to eschew all such properties entirely, no matter how alluring the promises, or how apparently well founded the venture. There are plenty of good listed securities, the prices of which periodically reach high and low points, the value of which is founded upon recognized business principles and necessities.

The listed securities of Wall Street are divided into two distinct classes: Industrial and Railroad; and viewed from a speculative standpoint the former class is the most hazardous, in that they are generally more subject to manipulation, competition, or harmful legislation. Those who possess a sufficiently tenacious speculative memory will recall the affairs of the Whiskey trust and the Cordage trust and their

sad demise; and while great declines, and even
assessments, have occurred in railroad stocks,
they have always eventually proved their real
value. Good Industrials may occasionally be
purchased safely and profitably, but the rails
present the same opportunities, and are safer
and more open to comprehensive investigation
and correct judgment.

At the rails, therefore, we stop. It may be
argued that the process detailed above is a matter of degree, and that it might be continued
until only government, or other gilt edged
bonds, remained; but the question here discussed is speculation, and it is taken for granted
that what is sought is the golden mean between
certain loss and certain cent per cent.; i. e. properties which combine a fair amount of stability
and future promise with periodical opportunities for advantageous purchases and sales.

Viewing the future of railroad securities in
a broad general light, their gradually increasing
value appears certain. The continued increase
of population produces for them present returns
from travel and shipping, and the demands of
the settled districts ensure more permanent returns. So far as probable competition is concerned, it grows daily less with the concentration of capital. It is likely that even today the

projectors of a railroad which would come into harmful competition with present lines would find it impossible to raise the money for the furtherance of their plan.

A brief perusal of statistics will show that the oldest and best railroad securities, representing the properties traversing a densely populated territory, are subject to the smallest comparative range of fluctuation. These stocks are gradually undergoing a process of absorption which will in time reach to the newer roads of less developed country.

The West, with its enormous undeveloped territory and resources, presents great promise to the prophetic mind. The problem of extensive irrigation is yet to be solved, but aside from agricultural pursuits, the West possesses a wealth of mineral and lumbering industries, and possibilities which independently guarantee its future.

"The Atchison Railroad is a streak of rust running through a desert," said the elder Woerishoffer thirty years ago, as he industriously sold the stock short at prices which would seem ridiculously low today. Possibly Atchison bore that aspect at that time, but today it is a modern, well equipped, dividend paying property, traversing a rich and constantly improving territory. The improvement of that brief period is significant.

The South also presents promise of great future improvement. The readjustment of cotton prices to a higher general level, and the development of important mineral resources are combining to dispel the long lethargy of this section, and the growing competitive importance of its gulf ports is too glaring to be misunderstood.

The believer in the continued growth and prosperity of the United States, the progress of the largely undeveloped West, and the awakening South may safely assume a gradual and rapid growth in the value of railroad securities of these sections. The consensus of intelligent opinion points to their long-continued improvement and advance.

The contention is therefore made and offered for consideration that the railroad properties of the West and South offer the best speculative opportunities, combined with the greatest degree of safety.

The foregoing will, possibly, appeal to the reader as looking rather to the long future of properties than to immediate speculative opportunities, but the fairness of the following statement must be admitted:

The hazards of speculation are so great that it is expedient to primarily consider a solid groundwork for ventures. The trader who deals in stocks, the future of which he considers secure, can operate more actively and courageously than under other circumstances. It does not follow that because he has faith in the long future of his chosen properties, he shall at once jump in and buy and await the accretion of time. The proposed plan of operation—to await low prices—is in no way changed by the cheerful view of the future.

Having formed a definite idea as to the general outlook of a certain group of properties, the investigator has narrowed his research to individual stocks. In this he will be guided by three periods—the past, present, and probable future.

In examining the history of a stock it will be found that in almost all cases the security has undergone, in early stages, a radical advance and decline. This is largely occasioned by the fact that the public always makes a favorite of a new security, and will participate freely in the affairs of an untried corporation, while standard issues go begging. This brings about a state of affairs already explained both technically and theoretically, and offers to the moneyed interests an opportunity to sell their holdings to the public at high prices, and recover them later at their own figures. Thereafter, the stock will probably take its place among the standards of the Street, and follows the general swing to high and low extremes with a gradual trend toward increased valuation.

Eliminating this abnormal period of initiation, the investigator will find a careful study of the past to be of great value. In all cases it will be found that earnings have gradually increased, allowing, of course, for abnormal periods of depression and inflation. The fixed charges and expenses have also increased, and by an examination of both these factors, as well as an allowance for the diversion of funds for purposes of purchase and improvement, which expenditures if intelligently made must add to the value of the property, the net result of the past may be considered a reasonable guide to future expectations.

The mere payment of dividends cannot be accepted as a safe basis of value, for dividends are often paid to the great detriment of the property, and on the other hand are frequently withheld when they might be safely paid. Earnings are the all important point, and when the investigator has answered to his satisfaction the questions, "What have they earned, and what have they done with the money?" he may consider himself well on the way to his goal.

With this record of the past formed, the present earnings may be scrutinized. They may recently have undergone a sudden advance out of proportion to normal growth, or vice versa. In either case a reversal of present conditions may be confidently expected.

This simple form of reasoning applied to the affairs of the United States Steel Company in 1901-1903 would have sounded a most distinct note of warning, the correctness of which has been amply demonstrated.

The probable future is based upon a gradual improvement from the normal value of the present as indicated by the past.

The consideration of assets, so far as a railroad property is concerned, must be founded principally on its ability to earn, and continue earning perpetually.

Minus its usefulness, the total assets of the greatest railway system in existence would be little better than a mass of old junk; but if a million dollars has been so expended as to bring a continued fair return, that amount may be considered an asset. The investigator therefore finds that his calculations must be based almost wholly upon the ability of a property to increase its earning power until territorial development reaches high tide, and thenceforth to maintain such earnings indefinitely.

It will not be necessary for the trader, personally, to compute the various and voluminous figures which show the net earnings—that is to say, the amount applicable to distribution to the various bond and stock holders. A comprehensive statement of income and expenditure may be obtained from different published statistical works, or by application to the secretary of the corporation in question. With these figures before him, the task of the student is one of examination rather than of compilation, and with such information at hand, the matter may be viewed in the same light as any other ordinary business transactions. The total income, less the fixed charges, is the amount applicable to dividends and surplus.

The man who undertakes such an investigation will be surprised at the ease with which he may arrive at interesting results.

The legal provisions of the company, the rights of holders of preferences, and of holders of common stock, etc., are all matters which should be examined, as they frequently have an important bearing on values.

If the plan mapped out has been intelligently followed, the investigator should, by comparing his result with the value of money, be able to judge of the normal value of any standard security. If his figures vary materially from the market price, and no important error nor omission has been made, the stock is selling either below or above a fair valuation, and the information which was the object of all his research has been gained. Possessed of this valuable knowledge, the speculator now turns his attention to the second phase of the question—the time to buy. It may be that the price of his favorite security is very low, but that a bad technical position exists which will warrant a belief in lower prices, or an extended period of dullness. This situation has already been sufficiently enlarged upon.

Recapitulating the matter offered above for consideration, the course recommended would appear as follows:

First, decision as to the securities to be dealt in, eliminating all wildcat and untried stocks, and choosing for operations standard listed securities.

Second, determining what stocks offer the

greatest promise of continued increase in value, as determined by territory and its probable development and growth.

Third, an examination of the physical and financial condition of the individual property, or properties, chosen, and a forecast of the probable future, based upon the demonstrated past.

Fourth, the fixing of a present normal value to be used as a pivotal point in actual operation.

Fifth, a consideration of the manipulative and technical conditions of the machine speculative in order to be able to judge of the more immediate action of the market. In other words, to locate the position of the stocks, whether in weak hands or strong.

This form of reasoning should not appear complicated; it is the same process which any business man would pursue in following a determination to enter the grocery business, and yet it may be emphatically stated that not one speculator in a hundred enters his field equipped with even the most desultory knowledge of what he is doing. Out of ten traders in U. S. Steel Preferred who were experimentally questioned two years ago, only half the number knew what the issue of preferred

stock amounted to; only two were aware of
the important fact that the dividend on the preferred stock was cumulative, and not one was
reasonably well posted as to its properties and
earnings.

And yet every one of these individuals could
adduce specious reasons why the stock should
advance or decline, reasons which at best were
incomplete, and at their worst, silly or false.
The outcome of their individual efforts has not
been followed, but it is safe to surmise that all
made mistakes which research, coupled with
intelligent judgment, would have prevented.

In the plan of study submitted in this
chapter, there will, no doubt, be a sense of in-
completeness, but the object has been rather
to guide the reader into a correct line of reasoning and investigating than to adduce
specific cases or pile up statistical proof.

Everything is left to individual effort and
judgment, and the man who begins the process
of research suggested will make rapid progress.   One developed fact will suggest another point to be investigated, and the process
will become interesting and profitable.

The man who studies and knows, is the only
man who makes permanent gains in speculation.

To those who refute the possibility of obtaining the necessary information for the forming of such opinions, or who consider the task too great or too complex for the ordinary mind, let the fair reply be made, "Try it." It is this hazy idea of mystery where none exists which deters the ordinary speculator from even attempting to use his own brains, and which leads him to base his operations upon hearsay or guesswork. Cases will occur where concealment, either partial or total, will be found. For such the remedy is simple: let these properties alone.

If the first step toward the investigation of the affairs of Amalgamated Copper had been taken, it would have appeared at once that the corporation was a mere shell, a holding company, and furthermore, a blind pool of the most pronounced type. The value of such knowledge employed in a negative sense, that is, in preventing operations in such hippodromed stocks, is a matter of history. The enormous public losses sustained in Amalgamated Copper would have been impossible in any business on earth except speculation, for in any other business affair examination would have been the first thought, and negotiations under parallel conditions would have been abruptly dropped.

It is not meant to say that a mere examination of figures and periods is by any means sufficient, but it is believed that once started in the correct path of examination and judgment, as opposed to the prevalent methods of guesswork and gambling, the trader will find ample opportunities and incentive for pursuing his researches to a logical conclusion. After this has been accomplished, success will be measured by his own capabilities and business acumen.

The chapter headed, "Analyzing Railroad Securities," in Mr. John Moody's book, "The Art of Wall Street Investing," will be of great assistance to the student who attempts to follow out the suggestions made above.

XIII

Conclusion

THE three stages necessary to the development of the theories advanced in this work were, first, a recognition of the fact that public ventures were, considered as a unit, generally disastrous; second, an analysis of the causes which were responsible for this unsatisfactory fact; and finally, a confirmation of such analysis by statistical exhibits.

Relative to the latter feature, the necessarily condensed and restricted nature of the figures submitted may be considered insufficient evidence, but as it is certain that there is never a material division of public speculative opinion at any time, the books of even one house with a public clientele may be considered a fair indication of all others.

If the four thousand accounts, with their tens of thousands of operations, could be presented in detail, this unanimity of action would be more apparent, and their barometrical value greatly magnified.

The figures submitted, however, are confirmatory and not basic, and while they are important, in that they dovetail with preconceived opinions, the logical conclusions presented must stand on their own bottom.

That the public loses money in speculation is a notorious fact; that such losses take place in an arena which presents equal opportunities for profit or loss is indisputable, and it must follow, as the night the day, that the losses sustained are the result of mistaken judgment, erroneous methods, or misleading appearances.

In presenting the different pitfalls which beset the path of the speculator, and suggesting a means of avoiding or bridging them, it is felt that a thorough understanding of such dangers was necessary to safety and maximum good results.

Fortified with a knowledge of the machinery of the speculative world, and its workings, the trader may indulge much more actively in his ventures than if he depended wholly upon even the most excellent judgment of intrinsic value. Thus the trader who is justified in believing general or individual current prices to be at low ebb, may act boldly and frequently with good results. He enters his campaign satisfied that material decline is improbable, that public liquidation is complete, and that the next important move will be upward. He brings to bear upon his operations his knowledge of technical conditions and natural market actions, and his foundation being secure, makes repeated successes. He bears constantly in mind the fact that a limit will eventually be reached, a fact which is easily submerged by undue enthusiasm, and he knows that it is far better to quit too soon than too late.

All these things are a distinct advantage in increasing profits and preventing loss, but they are of secondary importance. They are the branches, without which it is possible for the trunk to thrive, but which, themselves, will die if removed from the parent stem.

The great basic principle of speculation, the foundation upon which the entire structure rests, is the recognition of value. No sustained success is possible without this knowledge, and most failures are traceable to the lack of it. Yet so generally is this important element disregarded, or refuted, that we find it playing only a small part, or no part at all, in the operations of the average speculator.

In the speculative world we find many men capable of clear thinking, correct analysis, and sound business judgment falling over each

other in the rush to make purchases of properties of which they know nothing. The incentive to such purchase may be a whispered
tip, or contagious enthusiasm, and the ridiculous equation of luck plays no inconsiderable
part. The result is always the same.

To those who contend that all the obtainable
knowledge of speculative anatomy is limited
and unreliable, let this fair question be put:

Was there ever to your personal knowledge
a period of speculative extremes where all, or
most of the appearances and conditions herein
detailed did not exist in recognizable form?
To be more specific, when the public favorite,
U. S. Steel, was selling at its lowest prices were
not the technical appearances of dullness,
pessimism, and public disgust as distinct as
the activity and optimism had been at high
prices? And furthermore, were not the figures
by which an intelligent estimate of real values
and probabilities could have been demonstrated in the face of claims of watered stock,
lack of demand, and general decay, always
obtainable?

It was stated in the first chapter of this work
that the maximum result obtainable in such a
treatise would be the direction of thought into
proper channels. The theories, and even the

established facts advanced will no doubt meet
with opposition from that class of persons who
allow a general denial to take the place of
answering arguments, and who sniff at theo-
retical deductions. Such shallow reasoners
may at once be relegated to the ranks of the
numerous whist players who maintain and express an opinion that there is nothing in the
"book game," and who, in the face of overwhelming evidence that they are wrong, go on
losing games, and actually take pride in pro-
claiming to the world their benighted condition.

Theories, if correct, are embryotic facts, the
value of which lies wholly in their proper application, and no refutation, of even a faulty
theory, is worthy of consideration unless accompanied by answering argument.

There is, however, a large class of men capable of clear thought and sound judgment
who speculate unsuccessfully through allowing
these faculties to be contorted, or lie dormant
before the apparent mystery enveloping the
affairs of the bourse. The properly directed
exercise of the capabilities of these men would
soon rob the speculative arena of both its
mystery and its bugbears, and resolve it into

a place of business where extraordinary opportunities were annually presented.

To this latter class, the statements and deductions made herein are respectfully submitted.

INDEX